The International Legal Protection of Migrants at Sea

Comparative Discrimination Law

Volumes published in this Brill Research Perspectives title are listed at *brill.com/rpcds*

The International Legal Protection of Migrants at Sea

A Comparison of International, Regional and National Responses

By

Niba Fontoh

BRILL

LEIDEN | BOSTON

Library Congress Control Number: 2023947364

Typeface for the Latin, Greek, and Cyrillic scripts: "Brill". See and download: brill.com/brill-typeface.

ISSN 2667-3398
ISBN 978-90-04-68509-3 (paperback)
ISBN 978-90-04-68511-6 (e-book)

This book is printed on acid-free paper and produced in a sustainable manner.

Contents

Abbreviations

ACHR	African Convention on Human Rights
ATT	Arms Trade Treaty
CCPR	Convention on Civil and Political Rights
CFR	EU Charter of Fundamental Rights of the European Union
CPCR	Civilian Persons in Times of War
DTA	Declaration of Territorial Asylum
ECHR	European Court of Human Rights
ECRE	European Councils on Refugees and Exiles
EEZ	Exclusive Economic Zone
EXCOM	Executive Committee
FAL	Facilitation Committee
GTPRS	Guidelines on the Treatment of Persons Rescued at Sea
HCR	United Nations Human Rights Committee
ICCPR	International Convention on Civil and Political Rights
ILC	International Law Commission
IMO	International Maritime Organization
IOM	International Organization for Migration
ITLOS	International Tribunal for the Law of the Sea
LOSC	Law of the Sea Convention
MSC	Maritime Safety Committee
OAU	Organization of African Unity
OHCHR	United Nations Office of the High Commission for Human Rights
RCC	Rescue Coordination Centres
SAR	Safety and Rescue
SCIP	Sub coin on International Protection
SOLAS	International Convention for Safety of Life at Sea
UDHR	Universal Declaration of Human Rights
UNCLOS	United Nations 1982 Convention on the Law of the Sea
UNHCR	United Nations High Commission for Refugees
UNODC	United Nations Office on Drugs and Crime

The International Legal Protection of Migrants at Sea

A Comparison of International, Regional and National Responses

Niba Fontoh
Advanced Institute of Public Management, Bastos Nylon,
Yaounde Bastos, Yaounde, Cameroon
infos@ismp.com, nibafontoh@gmail.com, f.niba@icj-cij.org

Abstract

Faced with the migration crisis which has caused so many deaths of migrants at sea, this book addresses the issue by examining the international legal framework which enjoins States and other actors at sea to come to the rescue of migrants in distress at sea. The treatment of migrants at sea can unarguably be considered as biased and unequal with some migrants enjoying far more humane treatment than others owing to their status and other discriminatory criteria. This book seeks to provide a legal argument which obliges the international community to protect even illegal migrants who willingly and intentionally endanger their lives at sea, while ensuring that these rights and obligations are not abused. The protection of migrants at sea has been addressed by numerous international legal instruments and doctrine in varying legal domains of International Law like Maritime Law, Law of the Sea, International Human Rights Law, Humanitarian Law, International Criminal Law, International Refugee Law, and International Law against Transnational Organised Crime. This volume compares the protections required as well as their application by nations.

Keywords

migrants – protection – sea – maritime – international – law – treaties – states – obligations – responsibility

Introduction

Recently in the spring of 2023, over four hundred immigrants died at sea. Reports state that a plane administered by Frontex spotted a "heavily overcrowded" fishing boat "navigating at a slow speed" in the international waters

 | DOI:10.1163/9789004685116_002

near Greece. The Frontex plane notified Italian and Greek officials and monitored the boat for about ten minutes before returning to base for refuelling. Frontex claimed to have proposed additional support to the Greek authorities but received no response. Frontex also reported that the Greek authorities instead asked the agency to send a drone to another migrant rescue incident further east off the coast of Crete. The Greek Coast Guard claimed that it asked nearby vessels to assist the fishing trawler and one of them even reached the location on the 13th of June 2023 but claimed that the migrants had rejected their offer of assistance and said they wanted to continue their journey to Italy. In the morning of June 2023, Greek officials reported that the fishing boat capsized approximately 47 nautical miles from the coastal city of Pylos on the Peloponnese peninsula after the boat's engine failed. Survivors claim the Greek authorities tried to tow the boat leading to the engine failure and blame the Greek authorities, which was denied by the Greek authorities. As of the 28th of June, Greek authorities confirmed rescuing 104 survivors and recovering 82 bodies of migrants from Afghanistan, Egypt, Libya, Palestine, Syria and a town from Pakistan which had lost an entire generation of young men. At the time of this writing in June 2023, more than 47,000 refugees at sea had arrived by boat in the Mediterranean sea, up from about 18,000 refugees in the same period of 2022.[1]

On a closely related issue, Carola Rackete, the Master of the MV Sea Watch 3, was arrested on the 29th of June 2019 by Italian authorities for aiding and abetting illegal immigration and for forcing her way into the port of Lampedusa despite being denied authorization to disembark, and for causing damage to a police speedboat that tried to block her entry. She was carrying on board forty rescued migrants and had waited in international waters outside of Lampedusa for seventeen days whilst many of the migrants' physical and mental conditions deteriorated. Rackete had warned the Italian authorities that she feared for the safety of her vessel and those on board, but the Italian authorities maintained their stance of refusing disembarkation.[2]

Both these instances raise several issues with respect to the volition of humans to assist other humans in danger. Death at sea is no longer an effective deterrent for migrants in search of a better life abroad. The death toll

1 Reuters, Boat carrying 500 asylum seekers disappears in Mediterranean Sea (26 June 2023) *Aljazeera* <https://www.aljazeera.com/news/2023/5/26/boat-carrying-500-asylum-seekers-disappears-in-mediterranean-sea> accessed 30 June 2023.

2 Court of Agrigento, Judge's Office for Preliminary Investigations, Order of Request of Validation of Stop and Duty of Application of the Measure, article 391, in relation to articles 272 et seq. of the Italian Code of Criminal Procedure – the Judge of Preliminary Investigations, Dr. Ssa Alessandra Vella.

has become a collective concern for humanity in need of a global response. Unfortunately, the international community has witnessed numerous similar dramatic events unfolding in the high seas for the past two decades. The Mediterranean Sea has been the most popular passageway, yet constitutes the riskiest one for political refugees, civilians escaping war and even clandestine economic migrants in search of a receiving country.[3] This phenomenon of migration, however, is not new. In the past, men, women and children have embarked on risky life-threatening journeys by sea in search of employment, better living conditions, better education, or in search of international protection against domestic persecution or other threats on their lives, liberties or security.[4] Often such individuals are entrusting their lives into the hands of unscrupulous transporters and criminals.[5]

The sea has been very popular for migrations especially between the two Atlantics during large periods of history. The twentieth century phenomenon known as 'boat people',[6] originally referring to the mass exodus of Vietnamese fleeing domestic persecution in the 80s, followed by Albanians, Cubans, Haitians, etc., in the 90s, has however forged the vocabulary that has smuggled its way into our current language. Boat-People refers to persons with multifarious status, who leave their countries, for different reasons, trying to reach another country by ship, particularly coastal States in the Mediterranean, in the Caribbean-Sea or the Pacific Ocean.[7]

In comparison to migrations using roads as transport, migration by sea is more disturbing for at least two main reasons. First, the contemporary era has witnessed an increase in the adoption of drastic control measures limiting the entry of foreigners into their territories, be it maritime or by land. The major difference lies in the fact that land migrants can easily be repulsed to other

---

3 Patricia Mallia, 'Chapter 9: When Rights and Duties Collide: The Challenge Facing Malta in the Fight Against Irregular Maritime Migration', in Ivan Ureta and Derek Lutterbeck (eds), *Migration, Development and Diplomacy, Perspectives from the Southern Mediterranean* (The Red Sea Press Inc. 2010).

4 Ivan Selman Cooper, 'The New Boat People: Ensuring Safety and Determining Status' (January 2006) *Migration Policy Institute Report*.

5 IOM and UNHCR, *Rescue at sea – Handbook of principles and measures applied on migrants and refugees*, <https://www.unhcr.org/media/rescue-sea-guide-principles-and-practice-applied-migrants-and-refugees> accessed on 30 June 2023.

6 Marie-Laure Basilien-Gainche, 'Les Boat people de L'Europe. Que fait le droit ? Que peut le droit?' (2016) 2 *La Revue des droits de l'homme, Revue du Centre de recherches et d'études sur les droits fondamentaux*' 4.

7 See UNHCR, *Background Note on the Protection of Asylum-Seekers and Refugees rescued at Sea* (18 March 2002) http://www.unhcr.org/media/background-note-protection-asylum-seekers-and-refugees-rescued-sea accessed 30 June 2023.

territories in contrast to sea migrants, whose repulsion further endangers their lives. Second, sea migration is characterised by a colossal loss of human lives. The scenario in most cases is dramatic, especially in situations where the concerned persons face health challenges and are in urgent need of an amicable territory to receive them.[8] Thus, for more than three decades, Africa and other continents have continually paid the ultimate price for the phenomenon of sea migrations[9] evidenced by the loss of thousands of its sons and daughters who continually die in their quest for greener pastures and safety[10] through the Mediterranean Sea, onboard fortune vessels usually managed by ferrymen and abandoned in the coastal waters.[11]

This volume analyses the legal treatment by nations of migrants by sea, notably the question on the equality of treatment of these vulnerable migrants at sea by different countries, which raises serious political questions from a legal perspective. This approach is challenged by the thorny absence of any legal argument that obliges States to assist migrants who willingly and knowingly endanger their own lives by choosing to travel by sea despite the dangers. The demand for legal clarity in such situations is mostly made by actors who are regularly confronted with the problem of illegal migrants. This demand for such clarity can however be seen as threatening to eradicate any remnants of humanity still existing by creating a bright line that need not be exceeded. This demand for clarity probably would be reframed if those seeking such were at the other end of the challenge. Why should they rescue me if I am stranded at sea? Given that all human activities involve risk, it is only human to run for the assistance of those whose risk assessment proves faulty regardless of their status, while adopting measures to ensure that the humanity of one party is not abused by the other party in danger.

Faced with the current crisis, it is pivotal to recollect the ancestral rules and principles that enshrine 'solidarity' and can guide in the management of this

8 Geneviève Bastide-Burdeau, 'Migrations Clandestines et Droit de la Mer' in Laurent Luccinin and Jean-Pierre Queneuduc (eds.) *La Mer et son Droit – Mélanges Offerts* (Paris, Pedone 2003) 56–66, 56.

9 Valerie Blake, 'Mass African Migration into Europe – Human Rights and State Obligations' (2010) Vol. 32 *Journal of Public Law and Policy* 4.

10 From 2014–2018, more than 17,000 migrants were recorded as dead or missing in the Mediterranean Sea; International Organization for Migration, Missing Migrants Project <http://missingmigrants.iom.int> accessed 30 June 2023. From 2000–2018, more than 2,000 deaths were recorded in the South Pacific along the Australian boarders, Monash University, Border Crossing Observatory, Australian Border Deaths Database <https://www.monash.edu/arts/border-crossing-observatory/research-agenda/australian-border-deaths-database> accessed 30 June 2023.

11 Anete Bandone, 'Les Migrants en Méditerranée : la protection des droits de l'homme' (2015) *Direction Générale des Politiques Externes de L'Union, Département Thématique* 12–14.

humanitarian crisis.[12] In this light, even a summary analysis of the migration phenomenon reveals that the international law applicable to maritime migration is at the boundaries of numerous legal fields. This is because the ambits of the applicable law are found in the international law of the sea as well as international maritime law, from international refugee law to international human rights law, considering the fact that the phenomenon has hardly been treated for its own sake and remains at the peripheries of this group of rules. Even when acknowledged, the application of these rules most often has been confronted by variations in interpretation in need of clarification.

Despite the dispersed and subsidiary character of the applicable laws, an aspect of certainty can immediately be detected: migrants at sea enjoy some international legal protection regardless of their status.[13] In fact, international law consecrates, on one hand, the duty to assist all persons in danger at sea (I) and, on the other hand, refugee rights for all migrants travelling by sea, given the fact that their fundamental human rights remain untouched regardless of their status as 'sea' migrants (II).

This volume consists of two main sections; the first explores the legal arsenal on which the obligation to assist those in distress at sea is founded. Two of its parts outline the obligations of actors who are directly or indirectly involved in maritime activities; as well as the scope of their application, which is non-discriminatory and covers even the cases of smugglers and illegal migrants in distress. In essence, the first two parts define the behaviour of actors faced with migrants in distress at sea.

The second section sets out to clarify the comportment of rescuers after a rescue operation. This section contains four relatively shorter parts that are more analytical and seek to clarify concepts that often are interpreted with bias to the detriment of numerous migrants in distress. While Parts 3 and 4 clarify the behaviour of rescuers in the application of their duties, Parts 5 and 6 address institutional practices that undermine the safety of migrants in distress at sea such as the discriminatory practice of interceptions and refoulement on asylum seekers. The last part concludes with a prospective look at the theme of refugees at sea who are glaringly the most affected by the discriminatory practices.

---

12 See Yann Tephany, 'Sauvetage et migration maritime' (2015) *Programme Human Sea – Rendre la mer humaine* <https://www.monash.edu/arts/border-crossing-observatory/research-agenda/australian-border-deaths-database> accessed 30 June 2023.

13 See Anete Bandone, *Les migrants en Méditerranée : la protection des droits de l'homme* (Parlement européen – Direction générale des politiques extérieures – Département thématique, 2015), <https://www.europarl.europa.eu/RegData/etudes/STUD/2015/535005/EXPO_STU(2015)535005_FR.pdf> accessed 30 June 2023.

SECTION 1: THE OBLIGATION TO ASSIST THOSE IN DISTRESS AT SEA ENSHRINED IN INTERNATIONAL LAW

This section comprises two parts. The first examines the obligation to assist those in distress at sea both under International Maritime Law and the International Law of the Sea. This part clearly identifies the expected comportment of maritime actors faced with a ship in distress at sea in need of immediate intervention. The second part addresses efforts aimed at safe-guarding the obligation to assist even migrants in illegal situations or using unlawful methods of travel by sea like smuggling. The legal foundation of this situation is equally examined notably through the appropriate conventions.

Part 1: The Obligation to Assist under International Maritime Law and the International Law of the Sea

The two branches of international law most relevant to the issues addressed in this volume regarding refugees by sea, International Maritime Law,[14] and the International Law of the Sea,[15] set down explicit obligations incumbent on ship captains as well as obligations on all coastal States with respect to a duty to assist those at sea. The coastal States are charged with the responsibility of installing coordination services for the execution of research and rescue missions at sea.[16] The principal rules that govern this duty partly come from the international law of the sea and from international maritime law, but equally stem from the international law against the illicit traffic of migrants especially by sea: this is actually a residual rule that preserves this obligation even in favour of migrants within the framework of such traffic.

14 Maritime law, also referred to as admiralty law, is a body of laws, conventions, and treaties that govern private maritime business and other nautical matters, such as shipping or offenses occurring on open water <https://www.investopedia.com/terms/m/maritime-law.asp> accessed 30 June 2023.

15 The Law of the Sea is a body of customs, treaties and international agreements by which governments maintain order, productivity and peaceful relations on the Sea; National Ocean Service <https://oceanservice.noaa.gov/facts/lawofsea.html> accessed 30 June 2023.

16 Marc Lescaudron, 'Droit des réfugiés, droit des migrants, droit maritime: contraintes légales et cadre juridique du sauvetage des personnes en péril en Mer Méditerranée, le cas de SOS Méditerranée' (2016) *Prospective Coopération – Laboratoire d'idées* 11–12; <http://www.prospectivecooperation.org/wp-content/uploads/2017/10/EtudeDroitSOSM%C3%A9diterran%C3%A9e-ProspectiveWEB-1.pdf>, accessed 30 June2023.

1.1 *The Obligations Incumbent on the Master of Any Ship at Sea*

By virtue of an ancestral maritime tradition, as well as the obligations prescribed by international law, the captain of a vessel has a duty to assist all persons in situations of distress at sea, regardless of their nationality, status or even the conditions in which the person was found. The substantive form of this maritime norm in international law can be traced to the early part of the twentieth century. The Brussels Conventions of 23rd September 1910,[17] on The Unification of Certain Rules of Law Respecting Assistance and Salvage at Sea, and the other on Collision, legally consecrate this imperative. This text defines salvage as an obligation incumbent on the ship captain and reiterates, in its Article 11, that:

> Every member is bound, so far as he can do so without serious danger to his vessel, her crew and passengers, to render assistance to everybody, eventhough an enemy found at sea in danger of being lost. The owner of the vessel incurs no liability by reason of contravention of the above provision.[18]

To this effect, it is worth noting that the obligations incumbent on the masters of a ship can be comfortably organized under maritime law on one hand and law of the sea on the other hand.

1.2 *The Obligations under International Maritime Law*

The obligations examined in this section are drawn essentially from the body of laws, conventions and treaties that govern private maritime business and nautical matters. The use of maritime law in this situation is justified by the fact that the legal arsenal directly affects private actors who daily use the seas for commercial and other private purposes and are thus most likely to encounter migrants in distress.

17 Convention Internationale pour l'unification de certaines règles en matière d'assistance et de sauvetage maritimes. Conclue à Bruxelles le 23 Septembre 1910. Approuvée par l'Assemblée Fédérale le 17 Mars 1954. Instrument d'adhésion déposé par la Suisse le 28 Mai 1954 Entrée en Vigueur pour la Suisse le 15 Aout 1954.

18 The obligation of ship masters to provide assistance is repeatedly articulated in international maritime law. First codified in 1910, it is incorporated in Article 98 UNCLOS and Article 10 of the 1989 Salvage Convention. It is also explicitly mentioned in V7/ SOLAS. All three conventions require the master of a ship, so far as he can do so without serious danger to his vessel and persons thereon, to render assistance to any person in danger of being lost at sea and to proceed with all possible speed to the rescue of persons in distress. It is again specifically mentioned in (V/33) SOLAS but is not referred to in SAR, the emphasis of which is more on the responsibilities of States Parties to that Convention.

1.2.1 The Duty to Search and Rescue

The duty to rescue distressed persons at sea is backed by both humanitarian history and legal tradition.[19] This same duty to rescue is codified by both treaty and general international law,[20] and is applicable to both State vessels as well as private commercial vessels.[21] At the treaty level, rescue obligations extend to coastal States, flag States, and to shipmasters of commercial or merchant vessels. Coastal States Parties are required to arrange and coordinate effective search and rescue services, and flag States, coastal or otherwise, are required to enforce the rescue obligation among shipmasters. Shipmasters therefore have both an indirect duty to rescue, by virtue of flag State enforcement, and a direct duty under certain instruments.[22] Despite its vastness in ambit, ambiguity reigns in the interpretation of these legal instruments on rescue, thus contributing greatly to the weakening of the rescue regime. Rescue itself was only recently defined.

The notion of search and rescue has been prescribed in numerous international legal documents that can be very useful to defend the rights of migrants

---

19 *See* UNHCR ExCom, Problems Related to the Rescue of Asylum-Seekers in Distress at Sea, Conclusion No. 23 (XXXII) (Oct. 21, 1981) Conclusion No.23; *see also* UNHCR ExCom, Rescue of Asylum-Seekers in Distress at Sea, Conclusion No. 38 (XXXVI) (Oct. 18, 1985); Conclusion No. 38; UNHCR ExCom, Sub coin. On Int'l Protection 'SCIP', Problems Related to the Rescue of Asylum Seekers in Distress at Sea, EC/SCP/18 (Aug. 26, 1981) (describing the evolution of the rescue duty from its first emergence in an international instrument in 1910).

20 Convention on Salvage, Apr. 28, 1989, S. Treat Doc. No. 102-12 (1991), 1953 U.N.T.S.193 Salvage Convention; U.N. Convention on the Law of the Sea, Dec. 10, 1982, 1833 U.N.T.S. 397 (UNCLOS) (superseding the four 1958 Law of the Sea Conventions: Convention on the Territorial Sea and the Contiguous Zone, Apr. 29, 1958, 15 U.S.T.1606, 516 U.N.T.S. 205; Convention on the High Seas, Apr. 29, 1958, 13 U.S.T.2312, 450 U.N.T.S. 82; Convention on Fishing and Conservation of the Living Resources of the High Seas, Apr. 29, 1958, 17 U.S.T.138, 559 U.N.T.S. 285; Convention on the Continental Shelf, Apr. 29, 1958, 15 U.S.T.471, 499 U.N.T.S. 311); International Convention on Maritime Search and Rescue, Apr. 27, 1979, T.I.A.S. No. 11,093, 1405 U.N.T.S.97 (SAR); International Convention for the Safety of Life at Sea, Nov. 1, 1974, T.I.A.S. 9700, 1184 U.N.T.S. 278 (SOLAS). For a thorough overview of maritime treaty sources of the rescue obligation, *see* 'Chapter Eight: The Protection of Asylum-Seekers and Refugees Rescued at Sea' in Alexander Aleinikoff & Vincent Chetail (eds), *Migration and International Legal Norms* (The Hague; T.M.C; Asser Press, 2003).

21 UNCLOS obligates States Parties to enforce the rescue duty for *all* ships flying its flag including both commercial and State vessels. *See* Article 98(1) UNCLOS. SAR calls for coordination of search and rescue services using either designated 'rescue units' (public or private) or other (non-rescue) appropriate public or private services. *See* Chap. 2.4.1 SAR. Similarly, SOLAS requires States Parties to enforce rescue compliance by all of its shipmasters.

22 Articles 98(1) and (2) UNCLOS; Article 10 of the Salvage Convention, and Chapters 2–3 SAR.

at sea. Though not the pioneer legal instrument on search and rescue, the 1979 International Convention on Maritime Search and Rescue[23] enjoys the merit of succinctly defining these operations in its Annex. To this effect, Articles 1–9 of Chapter 1 treating terms and definitions, give an exhaustive definition of search and rescue operations that are judged worthy of complete citation for future clarity, stating that the terms listed below are used in the Annex with the following meanings:

1. 'Search'. An operation, normally coordinated by a rescue co-ordination center or rescue sub-center, using available personnel and facilities to locate persons in distress;
2. 'Rescue'. An operation to retrieve persons in distress, provide for their initial medical or other needs, and deliver them to a place of safety;
3. 'Search and rescue service'. The performance of distress monitoring, communication, co-ordination and search and rescue functions, including provision of medical advice, initial medical assistance, or medical evacuation, through the use of public and private resources including co-operating aircraft, vessels and other craft and installations;
4. 'Search and rescue region'. An area of defined dimensions associated with a rescue co-ordination center within which search and rescue services are provided;
5. 'Rescue co-ordination center'. A unit responsible for promoting efficient organization of search and rescue services and for coordinating the conduct of search and rescue operations within a search and rescue region;
6. 'Rescue sub-center'. A unit subordinate to a rescue co-ordination center established to complement the latter according to particular provisions of the responsible authorities;
7. 'Search and rescue facility'. Any mobile resource, including designated search and rescue units, used to conduct search and rescue operations; and
8. 'Search and rescue unit'. A unit composed of trained personnel and provided with equipment suitable for the expeditious conduct of search and rescue operations.[24]

---

23 The 1979 International Convention on Maritime Search and Rescue was adopted in Hamburg, Germany on the 27th of April 1979. This Convention dwells on search and rescue issues like; organization and coordination, cooperation between States, operating procedures, and ship reporting systems. The above factors judged indispensable for the effective execution of search and rescue operations.

24 Annex, Chapter 1, 1979 International Convention on Maritime Search and Rescue, Adopted in Hamburg, Germany on 27 April 1979.

The above provisions give a clearer content, context and even plan of action to any ship captain who is called upon to exercise the duty to search and rescue. With the above in mind, the duty to rescue incumbent on ship captains becomes clearer. It is in this spirit that numerous other international instruments, even those adopted before its coming into existence, perceived the duty to rescue people in distress as examined below.

The obligation is reiterated in Article 37 the International Convention for the Safety of Life at Sea (SOLAS).[25] SOLAS was the first international convention on the salvage of human life at sea adopted following the wreck of the *Titanic*, off the coast of Newfoundland, on the night of 14 and 15 April 1912, and has been amended several times before being completely rewritten in 1974. Regulation V/10 of the International Convention for the Safety of Life At Sea (LOS) of 1st November 1974, which came into force on the 25th of May 1980, also takes this up, stating that:

> [T]he master of a ship at sea, on receiving a signal from any source that a ship or aircraft or survival craft thereof is in distress, is bound to proceed with all speed to the assistance of the persons in distress informing them if possible that he is doing so. If he is unable or, in the special circumstances of the case, considers it unreasonable or unnecessary to proceed to their assistance, he must enter in the logbook the reason for failing to proceed to the assistance of the persons in distress.[26]

From the above regulation, not only is the master of the ship obliged to hastily run to the assistance of persons in distress, he is liable to some form of reproach if he fails to do so without tangible reasons that must be entered into the logbook.

Furthermore, The London Convention of 28 April 1989 on Salvage which entered into force on the 14 of July 1996, modernizes the regulations established by the Brussels convention of 1910 by stating in the first paragraph of its Article 10, that '[e]very master is bound, so far as he can do so without serious damage to his vessel and persons thereon, to render assistance to any person in danger of being lost at sea.' The imperative diction of Article 10 constitutes a

25 SOLAS aims at specifying a minimum standard for certain norms concerned with the construction and exploitation of commercial vessels, so as to guarantee the security of the crew, the passengers and the vessels. The sinking of the *Titanic* provoked this deep reflection on the security of maritime transport and a veritable international cooperation aimed at establishing the means put in place to ensure such a catastrophe does not happen again, *see* Scott Krist, *How the Titanic Changed Maritime Law* (24 July 2017) *Maritime Accidents, Maritime Law*.

26 Regulation V/10 of SOLAS.

glaring indicator to the desire to protect distressed victims, ensured by making the rescue operation an obligation on the master of the nearby vessel.

The United Nations Convention on the Law of the Sea, of 10th December 1982 (UNCLOS),[27] equally qualified this during the adoption of its 'Constitution for the Oceans'[28] which contains the most recent regulations on the duties incumbent on the master of the vessel in the domain of assistance. The first paragraph of its Article 98 states:

> Every State shall require the master of a ship flying its flag, in so far as he can do so without serious danger to the ship, the crew or the passengers:
> a) to render assistance to any person found at sea in danger of being lost;
> b) to proceed with all possible speed to the rescue of persons in distress, if informed of their need of assistance in so far as such action may reasonably be expected of him;
> c) after a collision, to render assistance to the other ship, its crew and its passengers and, where possible, to inform the other ship of the name of his own ship, its port of registry and the nearest port at which it will call.

Under SAR, search and rescue services must be established by States Parties and coordinated regionally to be capable of responding to distress signals in their particular rescue regions. As part of this, SAR calls for the designation of rescue units that are to participate in search and rescue functions at sea.[29] Perhaps even more importantly, the rescue regime foresees that where a designated rescue unit may not be available in the distress area, the relevant rescue coordinating center may properly designate a non-rescue vessel, public or private, to respond to the distress call,[30] or may even requisition a private vessel in the vicinity to participate in a particular rescue operation.[31] This position is further supported by UNCLOS which stipulates:

27 UNCLOS entered into force on the 16 of November 1994.

28 Tommy B. Koh, "*One Constitution for the Oceans*" (1982); https://www.un.org/depts/los/convention agreements/texts/koh french.pdf; accessed 30 June 2023.

29 The rescue units themselves may consist of 'State or other appropriate public or private services,' including warships, thus indicating that the rescue regime established by this treaty places no public/private restrictions on the nature of designated rescue vessels, see Sections 2.4.1.1 and 5.8.1 SAR.

30 Section 2.4.1.2 SAR.

31 This means that regional SAR coordination centers are vested with the authority to coordinate rescue arrangements among the most appropriate vessels in the rescue area, whether they are merchant vessels, specialized rescue vessels, or even warships, see Ch. V, reg. 33 SOLAS.

> Every coastal State shall promote the establishment, operation and maintenance of an adequate and effective search and rescue service regarding safety on and over the sea and, where circumstances so require, by way of mutual regional arrangements cooperate with neighbouring States for this purpose.[32]

Summarily, Article 98 UNCLOS can be said to contain two separate obligations that are addressed to two groups of States, namely the duty of flag States to oblige masters of vessels flying their flag to rescue people at risk of being lost at sea, and the duty of coastal States to maintain search and rescue services.

It should be born in mind that since 1956, the International Law Commission (ILC) considered its draft articles as codified custom.[33] Nowadays, it is generally accepted that Article 98 (1) and (2) UNCLOS reflects customary international law.[34] More recent doctrine adheres to this stance by agreeing that the duty to rescue persons in distress at sea is a fundamental rule of international law that has been incorporated into international treaties and forms the content of a norm of customary international law.[35] In the same light, its incorporation into numerous international and national legal instruments can be used to justify its status as one of the general principles of law mentioned in Article 38-(1) of the Statute of the International Court of Justice.[36]

The above international law instruments clearly make the duty to search and rescue an incumbent obligation on all ship masters. This obligation can be deduced to be of direct advantage and importance to migrants at sea. However, given the tendency of stakeholders to consciously derail the spirit of the law, it is paramount to delimit and clarify the scope of the duty to rescue from its *materiae* and *personae* perspectives. To this effect, it should be clearly stated that the duty to assist comprises all maritime zones. Article 98 UNCLOS is enshrined in Part VII which examines the high seas as well as the exclusive economic zone, based on Article 58(2). Given the muteness of the UNCLOS as concerns the territorial sea, the duty to assist can only be inferred from the

32 Article 98 (2) UNCLOS.

33 ILC, 'Articles concerning the Law of the Sea with Commentaries' (1956) Vol. 2 *Yearbook of the International law Commission* 281.

34 Richard Barnes, 'The International Law of the Sea and Migration Control', in Bernard Ryan and Valsamis Mitsilegas (eds.), *Extraterritorial Immigration Control: Legal Challenges* (Martinus Nijhoff 2010) 134.

35 Irina Papanicolopulu, 'The duty to rescue at sea, in peacetime and in war; A general overview' (2016) 98(2); *International Review of the Red Cross* 491–514; and *War and security at Sea* at 496.

36 Tullio Scovazzi, 'Human Rights and Immigration at Sea', in Ruth Rubio-Marin (ed.), *Human Rights and Immigration*; (Oxford University Press, Oxford 2014) 225.

reference to assistance in the case of distress as articulated in Article 18(2) UNCLOS.[37] In sharp contrast to UNCLOS, SOLAS evidently applies to vessels in all maritime zones.[38]

It should be equally underscored that the duty to render assistance is applicable to cases of collision between two vessels as well as situations where vessels receive information on the pending danger of being lost at sea because a vessel is in danger or sunken. This duty therefore is applicable, without distinction, to all persons in distress.[39] The all-encompassing text of the Article renders irrelevant the nationality of the vessels and persons concerned, their legal status as well as the activity in which they are involved. In other words, the illegal nature of an activity does not deprive the culprits of their right to be assisted in case of distress at sea. By deduction, the status of migrants should equally not nullify their right to be assisted or saved in case of distress. Unfortunately, certain States and masters of vessels have been observed to ignore distress calls from migrant or refugee-carrying vessels in violation of the above international legislation and other laws.[40]

As concerns the *rationae personae* scope of the duty to assist, it should be mentioned that the duty to rescue applies both to States and masters of ships although the UNCLOS only mentions the obligation of States. This is evidenced by the International Convention on Salvage[41] as seen above as well as the SOLAS Convention which stipulates that:

> The master of a ship at sea which is in a position to be able to provide assistance, on receiving a signal from any source that persons are in distress at sea, is bound to proceed with all speed to their assistance, if possible, informing them or the search and rescue service that the ship is doing so.[42]

37 John E. Noyes, 'The Territorial Sea and Contiguous Zone', in Donald R. Rothwell, Alex G. Oude Elferink, Karen N. Scott and Tim Stephens (eds.), *The Oxford Handbook of the Law of the Sea*; (Oxford University Press, Oxford 2015) 104.

38 Ch. 5, Regulation 1.1 SOLAS.

39 Chapter 2.1.10 SAR provides that '[p]arties shall ensure that assistance is provided to any person in distress at sea. They shall do so regardless of the nationality or status of such a person or the circumstances in which that person is found.' *See also* Regulation 33.1 SOLAS.

40 Interim Measures for Combating Unsafe Practices Associated with the Trafficking or Transport of Migrants by Sea, IMO Doc. MSC/Circ.896/Rev.1, 12 June 2001.

41 Article 10(1) SOLAS.

42 Regulation 33.1 SOLAS.

Furthermore, Article 98 UNCLOS can be considered as a general provision that comprises both military and civilian vessels, whether State-owned or private. Consequently, Article 98 UNCLOS is applicable to all ships without exception. This position is sharply opposed to the maritime conventions that explicitly exclude warships from their scope.[43] This perception of the duty to rescue is however excessively restrictive for two simple reasons, namely it diminishes the duty's underlying purpose that is to ensure that persons at risk of being lost at sea are saved, and secondly, because States are also bound by the duty to save lives at sea as enshrined in Article 98(2) UNCLOS. In fact, it would be highly contradictory for States to put in place search and rescue measures and services aimed at assisting those in distress, yet exempt their warships from offering such services.[44] In fact, no territorial justification supports this position. The UNCLOS further ameliorates this stance by expressly drafting the acceptable circumstances where a warship can be excluded from such duties like cases relating to the protection of the marine environment.[45]

Based on the above, it is neither absurd nor unfounded to strongly condemn warships and State vessels that fail to comply with their duty to save lives in distress at sea thus engendering international responsibility especially during peacetime. Since Article 98 UNCLOS envisages no exceptions, no such exceptions should be presumed. Again, engaged war vessels ought to avoid incidents and safeguard human life.[46] In fact, any lack of care resulting in maritime casualty should generate responsibility for the State and the persons involved.[47] This is however not the only obligation incumbent on the ship captain. Other duties are embedded in certain aspects treated herein below.

---

43 Article 14 of the 1910 Salvage Convention; and Article 4 of the International Convention on Salvage.

44 Irina Papanicolopulu, 'The duty to rescue at sea, in peacetime and in war: A general overview' (2016) 98(2) *International Review of the Red Cross* 491–514; and *War and security at Sea*, 496.

45 Article 236 UNCLOS.

46 A duty to ensure the safety of persons on board intercepted vessels is incorporated in, Article 9(1)(a) of the Protocol against the Smuggling of Migrants by Land, Sea and Air (Smuggling Protocol), supplementing the United Nations Convention against Transnational Organized Crime (UNTOC), 2241 UNTS 507, 15 November 2000 (entered into force 28 January 2004); and Article 8bis(10)(a)(i) of the Convention for the Suppression of Unlawful Acts against the Safety of Maritime Navigation, 1678 UNTS 201, 10 March 1988 (entered into force 1 March 1992), as modified by the 2005 Protocol.

47 This principle is illustrated by the case involving the Kater I Rades, which resulted in the condemnation of the master of an Italian warship that, through dangerous manoeuvres, had caused the sinking of the vessel Kater I Rades. See the decision of the Italian Court of Cassation of 10 June 2014, n. 24527. For a commentary on the case, see Tullio Scovazzi, 'Il respingimento di un drama umano collettivo e lesue conseguenze' in Amedeo Antonucci,

1.2.2 Rights and Duties with Regards to Illegal Migrants Generally

It is common knowledge that migrants travel in multifarious statuses. The two categories of pivotal concern to this section include the legal and illegal status of migrants. While it is logical to assume that the legal migrant is entitled to rights, duties and even privileges, it would be erroneous and even inhumane to perceive illegal migrants as migrants with neither rights nor duties worth enforcing due to their illegal status. As earlier mentioned in the introductory paragraphs, basic human solidarity warrants that these migrants be treated with dignity despite their illegal status. Besides, the status of illegality does not deprive them of their basic human rights as human beings.

To this effect, the rights and duties of illegal migrants can be treated from two perspectives as examined herein below.

1.2.3 The Protection of Illegal Migrants and Interception Measures

A trendy approach against protecting illegal migrants has been the absence of a legal argument to defend those who wilfully endanger their lives at sea. This however is a weak take that can be likened to saying that criminals do not have rights, which is a legal aberration notably from a human rights perspective. The fastest growing trend in maritime movements involves what has been termed 'mixed movements'.[48] The 1951 Convention relating to the Status of Refugees defines a refugee as someone who is unable or unwilling to return to their country of origin owing to a well-founded fear of being persecuted for reasons of race, religion, nationality, membership of a particular social group, or political opinion.[49] However, among seaborne migrants, there are also economic migrants looking for a better life in a developed country. As a result, states are quite reluctant to permit these persons onto their territory.

In order to prevent migrants from reaching their territory, states tend to take several interception measures at sea. Interception occurs when mandated authorities representing a state prevent embarkation of persons on an international journey, prevent further onward international travel by persons who

Irini Papanicolopulu and Tullio Scovazzi (eds.), *L'immigrazione irregolare via mare nella giurisprudenza italiana e nell'esperienza europea* (Giappichelli Editore Torino 2016).

48 Individuals or groups travelling in an irregular manner along similar routes and using similar means of travel, but for different reasons. This means that the people on board have various profiles and needs, as opposed to being primarily refugee outflows, see UNHCR, *All the Same Boat: The Challenges of Mixed Migration* (2016) <http://www.refworld.org/10pointplaninaction2016update.html-http://www.unchr.org/pages/4ald406060.hrml> accessed 30 June 2023.

49 Article 1 of the Convention relating to the Status of Refugees (adopted 28 July 1951, entered into force 22 April 1954) 189 *United Nations Treaty Series* 137 (Refugee Convention).

have commenced their journey, or assert control of vessels where there are reasonable grounds to believe the vessel is transporting persons contrary to international or national maritime law.[50] This can occur in the form of either physical interception or administrative measures. As a result, crossing the ocean becomes more difficult and migrants request the help of smugglers to reach their destination.

Due to the unlikelihood of return, most smugglers build boats with low-cost materials and finance the fuel for a return trip with more people, thus resulting in more drowning. The Maritime Safety Committee (MSC) of the International Maritime Organization (IMO), observed that illegal migrants are often transported on ships that are not properly manned, equipped or licensed for carrying passengers on international voyages and that states should take steps to eliminate these unsafe practices.[51]

When a person is in distress at sea, it is a legal obligation for shipmasters and states under customary international law, as well as under Articles 58(2) and 98(1) UNCLOS, to render assistance and to proceed, with all possible speed, to the rescue of persons in distress. Although UNCLOS only mentions this duty in application to the exclusive economic zone (EEZ) and on the high seas, a state cannot rely on its sovereign powers to disregard this obligation in its territorial sea. As assistance must be given to any person, the obligation applies regardless of the persons' nationality or status or the circumstances in which they are found. Rescue also implies that persons in distress have to be delivered to a place of safety. The IMO Guidelines on the Treatment of Persons Rescued at Sea state that a place of safety can be defined as a location where rescue operations are considered to terminate, where the survivors' safety or lives are no longer threatened, basic human needs (such as food, shelter and medical needs) can be met, and transportation arrangements can be made for the survivors' next or final destination. As smugglers are generally well informed about states' protection obligations and act to exploit them, they are able to instruct migrants on what to do upon interception to increase their chances of gaining entry into, and remaining in, countries of destination.

The rights and duties that can be attributed to coastal States and smuggled migrants can most conveniently be situated with the entry into force of the Protocol Against Smuggling[52] wherein, 'maritime interception was implic-

50 UNHCR, 'Conclusion on Protection Safeguards in Interception Measures,' EXCOM Conclusion No. 97 (LV) (2003).

51 Paragraph 4, Interim Measures for Combating Unsafe Practices Associated with the Trafficking or Transport of Illegal Migrants by Sea (MSC), MSC.1/Circ. 896/Rev. 1 (12 June 2001).

52 See generally, United Nations Convention Against Transnational Organized Crime (UNTOC) and the protocols 2004.

itly acknowledged as a legitimate tool for border control and enforcement.' Article 8 of the Protocol allows the search, boarding, and seizure of persons and cargo where there are reasonable grounds to suspect that the vessel is engaged in smuggling:

> A State Party that has reasonable grounds to suspect that a vessel exercising freedom of navigation in accordance with international law and flying the flag or displaying the marks of registry of another State Party is engaged in the smuggling of migrants by sea may so notify the flag State, request confirmation of registry and, if confirmed, request authorization from the flag State to take appropriate measures with regard to that vessel. The flag State may authorize the requesting State, inter alia:
> a) To board the vessel;
> b) To search the vessel; and
> c) If evidence is found that the vessel is engaged in the smuggling of migrants by sea, to take appropriate measures with respect to the vessel and persons and cargo on board, as authorized by the flag State.[53]

In this instrument, interception is contemplated in a more cooperative context, where flag States may grant authorization to foreign-flagged State vessels in order to facilitate interception of suspected smuggling vessels.[54] This provision effectively dispenses with the concept of exclusive flag State jurisdiction by creating an interception-sharing scheme where authorized by the flag State. These provisions are exclusive to the maritime context of the Protocol, and include particular safeguards that include obligations to ensure the safety and humane treatment of persons on board and not to endanger the security of the vessel or its cargo. In fact, the text presents a more eloquent expression of these obligations:

> Where a State Party takes measures against a vessel in accordance with article 8 of this Protocol, it shall:
> a) Ensure the safety and humane treatment of the persons on board;
> b) Take due account of the need not to endanger the security of the vessel or its cargo;
> c) Take due account of the need not to prejudice the commercial or legal interests of the flag State or any other interested State;

53 Article 8.2 of the Smuggling Protocol.
54 Articles 8.3 and 8.4 of the Smuggling Protocol.

d) Ensure, within available means, that any measure taken with regard to the vessel is environmentally sound.[55]

Additional protection for those found aboard smuggling vessels is provided by a savings clause preventing any Protocol provisions from infringing upon rights guaranteed under international humanitarian law, international human rights law, the Refugee Convention, and the principle of *non-refoulement* as contained therein.

> Nothing in this Protocol shall affect the other rights, obligations and responsibilities of States and individuals under international law, including international humanitarian law and international human rights law and, in particular, where applicable, the 1951 Convention2 and the 1967 Protocol3 relating to the Status of Refugees and the principle of non-refoulement as contained therein.[56]

This is an important provision given the growing recognition that refugees, with increasing prevalence, are now resorting to smuggling as a means of escaping persecution and reaching safer territory. These provisions require corresponding guidelines to safeguard the rights of intercepted persons in need of international protection vis-a-vis the intercepting State. An implied aspect of protection can equally be deduced from the contents of Article 6 of the Protocol which seeks to criminalize the act of smuggling.

Efforts aimed at improving safeguards in the rescue context have been both considerable and promising. This is evidenced by the increasing reactions of the international community since 2002 to treat the disembarkation subject by harping on specific issues alongside accompanying guidelines that entered into force in July 2006.[57] At the Expert Roundtable in Lisbon later in 2002, the 'next port of call' recommendation was discarded and replaced with a recommendation to increase '*shipmasters' discretion*' in determining the time and place for disembarkation, although ultimately no firm rule was recommended. Instead of adopting forceful language to encourage the establishment of a

55 Article 9.1 of the Smuggling Protocol.

56 Article 19.1 of the Smuggling Protocol.

57 In 2002, UNHCR revived discussions on the issue of protection for asylum seekers and refugees rescued at sea. In a 2002 Background Note, UNHCR confirmed the 'lack of clarity' in maritime law with regard to disembarkation, revived its call for prompt disembarkation at the *next port of call*, and recommended that screenings for refugees be performed on dry land rather than onboard a vessel, reasoning that prompt disembarkation would be more likely to lead to timely screenings, processing, and protection access.

new practice, the Roundtable merely observed shipmasters' 'right *to expect the assistance of coastal States*,' and called upon coastal States to *provide assistance* where requested by rescue vessels. Worthy to note was the yawning absence of criteria to determine the State or States responsible for disembarkation, screening, and access to asylum procedures, temporary protection and resettlement. Ultimately, the Roundtable conclusions failed to definitively resolve the disembarkation issue, although the suggestion to respect shipmasters' discretion created a potential starting point.[58]

In May 2004, the IMO adopted amendments to both the SOLAS and SAR Conventions, and created a set of *Guidelines on the Treatment of Persons Rescued at Sea*;[59] which address, among other things, the disembarkation issue. The two sets of amendments entered into force on 1 July 2006, and contain a nearly identical provision for identifying the coastal State responsible for disembarkation. Parties shall co-ordinate and co-operate to ensure that masters of ships providing assistance by embarking persons in distress at sea are released from their obligations with minimum further deviation from the ships' intended voyage, provided that releasing the master of the ship from these obligations does not further endanger the safety of life at sea. The party responsible for the search and rescue region in which such assistance is rendered shall exercise primary responsibility for ensuring such coordination and co-operation occurs, so that survivors assisted are disembarked from the assisting ship and delivered to a place of safety.[60]

Consideration should be given to specificities of the case and guidelines developed by the organization. In these cases, the relevant parties shall arrange for such disembarkation to be effected as soon as reasonably practicable. Interestingly, the IMO amendments reflect neither the United Nations High Commission for Refugees ('UNHCR') Background Note recommendation to vest the disembarkation duty with the 'next port of call' State, nor the muddled Roundtable approach to merely respect shipmasters' discretion as to where disembarkation should occur. Instead, primary authority for disembarkation

58 A much more tangible and promising consequence of the Roundtable resulted from its follow-up efforts with the IMO. As the UN agency primarily responsible for issues of maritime safety, the IMO is the drafting and amending body of SAR and SOLAS, the latter instrument being the principal international treaty concerned with the safety of merchant ships. One of the follow-up goals of the 2002 Lisbon Round Table was to encourage the IMO to address 'any inadequacies in the law' and identify the drafting inadequacies of the treaty instruments pertaining to rescue.

59 'Guidelines on the Treatment of Persons Rescued at Sea,' MSC Resolution 167(78) (20 May 2004), Annex 34, para. 6.12.

60 Chapter 17 SARS.

decisions lies with the State responsible for search and rescue in the region where the rescue occurs. What this means in practical terms is that the Rescue Co-ordination Centers ('RCCS') may now designate where disembarkation will occur on behalf of the assisting vessel, regardless of the status of that vessel as private or State-owned, military or non-military. It remains to be seen how this new disembarkation scheme will affect rescue in practice. In theory, conferring the disembarkation decision on the State responsible for the rescue coordination represents a practical solution, while potentially involving prospective risks in actual implementation.

Perhaps even more consequential than the amendments are the accompanying *Guidelines on the Treatment of Persons Rescued at Sea*. This instrument is designed to provide guidance to States Parties to SAR and/or SOLAS and to shipmasters with regard to humanitarian obligations and obligations under the relevant international law relating to treatment of persons rescued at sea. It attempts to address many important issues that are conspicuously missing from the maritime treaty amendments, including, for example, clarification of the meaning of place of safety. The *Guidelines* do not attempt to provide a singular definition of the concept of place of safety, but they do give insight into its meaning. For example, a place of safety is a 'location where rescue operations are considered to terminate, and from which survivors' safety and basic human needs can be met'. It can also be a very temporary transit point, however, since it is also 'a place from which transportation arrangements can be made for the survivors' next or final destination'.

Moreover, under the *Guidelines*, a place of safety may not even necessarily be on dry land; it may be aboard a rescue unit or other suitable vessel or facility at sea that can serve as a place of safety until the survivors are disembarked to their next destination. This poses an immediate problem of robbing the new amendments of any meaningful improvements, since they require that survivors be disembarked from the assisting ship and delivered to a place of safety. If disembarkation from one ship can simply mean delivery to another vessel, then clearly the disembarkation problem has not been solved. It is thus clear that a place of safety is a much narrower and more limited concept than that of disembarkation, and that the potential for survivors to languish on board a vessel remains a risk.

The *Guidelines* also discuss the potential conflict between the need to promptly disembark rescued persons and States' non-rescue-related interests in screening such individuals before permitting disembarkation. On this matter, the *Guidelines* are clear that delivery to a place of safety should take precedence over any non-SAR concerns, and that these should not delay disembarkation: Any operations and procedures such as screening and status assessment of rescued persons that go beyond rendering assistance to persons in distress should not be allowed to hinder the provision of such assistance or unduly delay disembarkation of survivors from the assisting ship(s).

This notion suggests that concern over a rescued individual's refugee status may not be used as grounds for delaying disembarkation. It also implies that the State of disembarkation retains responsibility for screening of rescued persons, since any State concerns over status assessment must necessarily follow disembarkation. In this sense, it suggests that responsibility for screening (to identify rescued persons in need of international protection) lies with the State of disembarkation. The SAR and SOLAS amendments offer promising new changes to the rescue instruments by finally making the disembarkation duty the explicit responsibility of the RCCs. The accompanying *Guidelines* offer new insight into the meaning of 'place of safety' and permissible bases for delaying disembarkation of rescued persons. One problem with the *Guidelines*, however, is its legal status as a non-binding instrument.

Lastly, States and other stakeholders are developing a disturbing trend of characterizing interceptions as rescue operations. At a May 2006 meeting of State representatives convened by UNHCR to discuss maritime interception and rescue in the Mediterranean basin, concern was raised over 'the practice whereby several States were classifying some interception measures as rescue at sea operations, in order to use SAR operational capacity for such activities.

When, then, is it a rescue, rather than an interception? The answer may lie partly in the motives underlying State practice. In the first place, calling an act a 'rescue' provides an instant legal basis to interfere with another vessel, particularly on the high seas, where the limited 'right of visit' exceptions may be otherwise unavailable. In short, if a flag vessel is clearly from another flag State, and not under suspicion of smuggling or piracy, no interference with a vessel is permitted without the flag State's express authority, unless it is in distress. The combination of the remote and unsupervised high seas locale combined with increased State pressure to intercept makes rescue a more tempting justification for interference on the high seas. The trend is also emerging in response to the relative ease with which rescue vessels can be discharged of further responsibility following disembarkation. Due to the very recent changes to the rescue regime designed to improve the efficiency of rescue disembarkations, the problem of 'cloaked' interceptions is likely to get worse. This is because a rescue operation on the high seas now affords prompt disembarkation coordinated by a third party (the regional RCC), whereas a high seas interception affords no clear responsibilities to discharge a protection responsibility. The temptation to characterize an interception as a rescue is therefore strong. Rescue at sea by a State's military vessels can and does occur under legitimate circumstances, and the SAR Convention contemplates such vessels playing a valid role in maritime search and rescue.

Today, it is not uncommon for a State's marine military service to be vested with twin rescue and interception duties, like the U.S. Coast Guard is one such example. But what happens when a dual service State vessel identifies an unseaworthy boat under reasonable suspicion of smuggling? Is the unseaworthiness of the craft enough to justify a rescue, or is the strong suspicion of smuggling more determinative of an interception? The response would dictate disembarkation and protection responsibilities for those on board, given that SAR and SOLAS amendments have created one disembarkation scheme for rescue victims, and the ExCom Conclusion has proposed a separate disembarkation and protection responsibility scheme for intercepted persons.

There remains pervasive confusion as to the distinction between rescue and interception in certain contexts.[61] Listed among the factors motivating interception is, 'the humanitarian imperative to come to the aid of those travelling in unseaworthy vessels,' which 'constitutes an added element of interception practices. Such a position is also taken by the U.S. Coast Guard, for example, which characterizes its Alien Migrant Interdiction program as involving '*primarily*' a 'humanitarian responsibility to prevent the loss of life at sea, since the majority of migrant vessels are dangerously overloaded, unseaworthy or otherwise unsafe'. Such language clearly equates interception with an underlying humanitarian-based rescue objective. If the ExCom position is that vessels responding to persons in distress at sea are *not* engaged in interception, how can *interception* include the humanitarian imperative to aid those in unseaworthy vessels? These seemingly irreconcilable positions were recognized by the Expert Roundtable convened in Athens to discuss interception and rescue in the Mediterranean basin, but no concrete proposals were put forward to address the problem.

At present, one clear source of guidance appears to be the ExCom *Conclusion on Protection Safeguards in Interception Measures*, which observes in its preamble that 'when vessels respond to persons in distress at sea, they are not engaged in interception'. This provision implies that distress is determinative of rescue, yet an ambiguity remains over the meaning of the term 'distress,' and the fact that it is frequently conflated with 'unseaworthiness' in the maritime context, which is inappropriate. Under a strict reading of this authoritative,

61 In a September 2005 *Background Paper for an Expert Round table on Rescue at Sea and Maritime Interception in the Mediterranean*, UNHCR provided a brief overview of the 'range of concerns and objectives' motivating States to intercept.

but non-binding clause, *any* encounter with a migrant vessel in distress should be characterized as a rescue. Apparently, not even UNHCR is very clear about how this issue is to be interpreted. More helpful, perhaps, is the SAR definition of a distress phase, which may shed some light on the more technical meaning of distress itself. The distress phase is defined as: 'A situation wherein there is reasonable certainty that a person, a vessel or other craft is threatened by grave and imminent danger and requires immediate assistance'.[62]

The 'reasonable certainty' characteristic of the distress phase is distinguished from other phases that are characterized by either uncertainty or apprehension as to the safety of the vessel. This language clearly implies that the unseaworthiness of a vessel is, after all, a matter of degree, and in order to justify a bona fide rescue operation, there must be reasonable certainty of grave and imminent danger. The recent trend of States characterizing interception operations as rescue is a dangerous one.[63] It threatens not only to weaken the rescue regime by burdening coastal States with undue disembarkation (and screening) responsibility, but constitutes a real risk that persons deserving of international protection will be exposed to harm. A greater clarification of the boundaries and distinctions between rescue and interception is necessary to stem the abuse, and a logical starting point is perhaps the SAR definition relating to distress. These are however treated in the ensuing sections of this work. It is imperative to examine the protection measures for migrants at sea through human rights instruments.

1.2.4 Migrants at Sea and the Respect for Human Rights

It should be highlighted that whatever their nationality or legal status, migrants at sea are equally protected by an impressive number of international and regional legal instruments that protect their human rights just as for all other human beings. These are examined below in three categories, international human rights instruments, regional human right instruments, and human right as addressed in other international and regional instruments.

62 1979 International Convention on Maritime Search and Rescue (SARS), Annex, Chapter 1, 1.3.13.

63 Felix Vacas Fernandez, 'The European Operations in the Mediterranean Sea to deal with Migration as a Symptom; and the Italian Operation Mare Nostrum to Frontex operations Triton and Poseidon, EUNAVFOR-MED and NATO's assistance in the Aegean Sea' (2016) 20 SYIL 93–118, 97.

1.2.4.1 *International Human Rights Instruments*

The overarching instrument at the international level is unarguably the Universal Declaration of Human Rights[64] (UDHR). Without ignoring the insightful words of the preamble that apply squarely to migrants at sea, it is pivotal to cite the precise articles of this instrument that merit particular attention where the protection of migrants at sea is to be taken seriously. In this light, the UDHR stipulates clearly that 'everyone has the right to life, liberty and security of person'.[65] This Article clearly counters the lack of liberty and security endured by migrants that has led to, and continues to destroy the lives of migrants in the seas every year.

Furthermore, the UDHR evokes a right whose violation has led to an even higher loss of migrant lives at sea. To this effect, it lays down in clear terms that '[n]o one shall be subjected to torture or to cruel, inhuman or degrading treatment or punishment'.[66] The ordeal of migrants at sea needs no belabouring. The savage treatment meted on migrants at sea on board smugglers' ships could not receive a more effective rebuke. Lastly, enshrined in the UDHR is the pivotal right of movement whose lack of application is deliberately flaunted by most government authorities or states whose domestic and international policies strive to protect their local socio-economic and political integrity. Thus, the UDHR inscribes in its Article 13 that '[e]veryone has the right to freedom of movement and residence within the borders of each state' and that '[e]veryone has the right to leave any country, including his own, and to return to his country'.[67] The pertinence of these articles is further strengthened when read in harmony with the ensuing paragraph that reads that '[e]veryone has the right to seek and to enjoy in other countries asylum from persecution'.[68] The protection offered by these articles traverses all socio-political and economic barriers established by states that seriously violate the rights of humans in general and sea migrants in particular. These articles place great rights and duties on those coastal States engaging in the systematic refoulement of migrants seeking safety in their land whatever their status.

A second very important legal instrument that can be used to enhance the protection of migrants at sea from a human rights perspective is the

---

64 The United Nations General Assembly' Universal Declaration of Human Rights' (UDHR) 10th December 1948, A/RES/217 (UDHR). Despite its status as a non-obligatory legal instrument, the dispositions of the UDHR are generally reputed as an integral part of international customary law.

65 Article 3 UDHR.

66 Article 5 UDHR.

67 Article 13 (1) and (2) UDHR.

68 Article 14 (1) UDHR.

International Covenant on Civil and Political Rights (ICCPR)[69] which was signed and ratified by all UN member states. The ICCPR equally surfs on the same waves as the UDHR, especially in relation to the right to life, stating that '[e]very human being has the inherent right to life. This right shall be protected by law. No one shall be arbitrarily deprived of his life'.[70] The inhumane treatment of humans is also addressed, stating that '[n]o one shall be subject to torture or to cruel, inhuman or degrading treatment or punishment. In particular, no one shall be subjected without his free consent to medical or scientific experimentation.'[71] As well is the right to free movement as laid down by Article 12 ICCPR.

The United Nations Human Rights Committee (HRC), which is a control organ of the ICCPR, declares that 'member states should not expose individuals to risks of torture, pain or cruel treatment which is inhuman or degrading by sending them back to another country by virtue of extradition, expulsion or refoulement'.[72] The HRC equally highlights the obligations of State Parties as laid down in Article 2 ICCPR, demanding that State parties respect and guarantee that all persons found on their territory and those under their control will enjoy the rights enshrined in the Pact and accept the obligation not to extradite, displace, expulse, or transfer someone by other means from their territory if there are serious reasons to believe that they run a real risk of irreparable prejudice in the territory to which they are being sent, or to any country in which the concerned person can be sent back. Such prejudices are envisaged in Articles 6 and 7 ICCPR.[73]

Again, the Convention on the Rights of the Child (CRC) equally acknowledges that every child has an inherent right to life, stating that 'States Parties recognize that every child has the inherent right to life.'[74] This inherent right to live is further buttressed by Article 37 CRC which procures further protection for children against inhuman or degrading treatment:

69 International covenant on Civil and Political Rights (ICCPR), 16 December 1966, 999 UNTS 171.

70 Article 6 (1) ICCPR.

71 Article 7 ICCPR.

72 Human Rights Committee (HRC), general observation number 20, Article 7 (Prohibition and Torture, Other Cruel, Inhuman or Degrading Treatment or Punishment, 10 March 1992, <https://www.refworld.org/docid/453883fb0.html> accessed 30 June 2023; and UN Doc HRI/GEN/1/Rev.1, paragraph 9.

73 Human Rights Committee, General Observation No. 31, 'La nature de l'obligation juridique general impose aux Etats parties au Pacte', 26 May 2004, UN Doc CCPR/C/21/Rev.1/Add.13, paragraph 9.

74 Article 6(1) CRC; and General Assembly Resolution 44/25 of 20 November 1989, and entry into force 2 November 1990.

> States Parties shall ensure that; No child shall be subjected to torture or other cruel, inhuman or degrading treatment or punishment. Neither capital punishment nor life imprisonment without possibility of release shall be imposed for offences committed by persons below eighteen years of age[75]

It is worth mentioning that Article 37 (a) CRC tallies tightly with the circumstances surrounding the treatment of migrants at sea who regularly suffer heart-rending treatment from their unscrupulous transporters and even state parties who send back desperate migrants to their death by denying them access to places of safety. Within the framework of the above articles, The Committee on the Rights of the Child proposes a wider interpretation that forbids the refoulement of children from a country if there are serious reasons to believe in the existence of a real risk of irreparable damage.[76] The last international instrument that can be effectively mobilized to ensure the protection of the fundamental human rights of migrants by sea is the convention against torture which is treated in detail in the subsequent parts.

1.2.4.2 *Regional Human Rights Instruments – European Law*

It would be illogical to side-line the regional efforts made by the European Union to ensure the protection of human rights that can be stretched into the domain of protection for migrants at sea. To this effect, the inevitable documents include the European Convention on Human Rights (ECHR)[77] and the Charter of Fundamental Rights of the European Union (CFREU).[78] These legal instruments apply on the institutions and member States of the European Union indiscriminately in their application of the European Union law.

A panoramic view of both the ECHR and CFREU exhibit pertinent human rights principles that are applicable to migrants who arrive to Europe through the Mediterranean Sea, as well as on acts by member states of the Union out of their territory, notably the sea. The right to life logically takes first place in both documents.[79] Without harping any further on the vocabulary that is

75 Article 37 (a) CRC.

76 United Nations Committee on the Rights of the Child, General Observation number 6 on the treatment of unaccompanied minors and children separated outside their country of origin, 1st September 2005, UN Doc CRC/GC/2005/6, paragraph 27.

77 Convention on the protection of human rights and liberties, 4th November 1950, 213 UNTS 222.

78 Ratified on the 26th of October 2012.

79 Article 2 (1) CFREU and ; Article 2 ECHR.

reproduced *mutatis mutandis* from similar human rights legislation, emphasis should be laid on the implications that discourages the disproportionate resort to force as a means of preventing the entry of migrants into their territory especially if the migrants are judged to have an illegal status. Within this context, the right to life is interpreted as an obligation to assist persons in distress in the sea. An equally important aspect enshrined in these human rights documents of the European Union forbids the torture, inhuman or degrading treatment of people. In this regard, both documents state in exactly the same wordings, that '[n]o one shall be subjected to torture or to inhuman or degrading treatment or punishment'.[80]

Both instruments require an absolute restriction that should be highlighted. Thus, the liability of the Union and its member States can be engaged even for acts accomplished out of their respective territories. By extension, cooperation agreements between the Union and its member States on one hand, and third-party countries on the other hand, to secure their borders and expulse or keep illegal migrants at bay by means of coercive measures, should be executed within the ambits of Articles 3 and 4 (ECHR and CFREU) of these legal texts that demand the respect of human dignity and the protection of persons who risk persecution in their countries of origin or transit countries.

In conformity with the Geneva Convention of 1951 and its 1967 protocol, the right to asylum cannot be neglected. Article 18 CFREU states in blatant terms that the 'right to asylum shall be guaranteed with due respect for the rules of the Geneva Convention of 28 July 1951 and the Protocol of 31 January 1967 relating to the status of refugees and in accordance with the treaty establishing the European Community.' Curiously, the ECHR does not address the case of asylum for the simple reason that for asylum issues during the said era, the Geneva Convention of 1951 was regarded as an authority in everything concerning the rights of refugees.

Another equally fundamental issue addressed by the ECHR and the CFREU is the express prohibition of collective expulsion of foreigners. While the ECHR treats the prohibition of slavery and forced labour,[81] it does so in very general terms despite its importance in this particular context. The CFREU on the other hand, grants an adapted and immediately useful legislation to the context of migrant protection in the seas. Under Article 19 CFREU entitled 'Protection in

80 Article 4 CFREU and Article 3 ECHR.
81 Article 4 ECHR.

the event of removal, expulsion or extradition', it is clearly stated that collective expulsions are prohibited.[82] The ensuing paragraph elucidates even further:

> No one may be removed, expelled or extradited to a state where there is a serious risk that he or she would be subjected to the death penalty, torture or other inhuman or degrading treatment or punishment.[83]

The ambits of this provision were clarified by the European Court of Human Rights (ECtHR) in the case of *Hirsi Jamaa and Others vs Italy*, wherein, the Court ruled that even 'acts accomplished outside the national territory, like interceptions and debarkations of migrants arriving by sea into a third country, without an individual examination of each case, can be likened to a collective expulsion'.[84]

It is equally worth noting that despite the almost explicit absence of the principle of non-refoulement by ECHR, the ECtHR ruled in the famous case of *Soering* that the expulsion of an individual can raise a problem with regards to Article 3 ECHR, thus engaging the liability of Member States to the Convention, especially when there is a serious and verified reason to believe that the concerned, if returned, will be exposed to a palpable risk of torture, punishment or other inhuman treatment.[85]

Although the application of these human rights instruments can be logically restricted to the jurisdiction of the contracting states, Article 1 ECHR mandates that all contracting parties acknowledge and pledge to respect these rights and liberties in relation to all persons found within their jurisdiction. To this effect, the ECtHR gives a predominantly territorial definition of jurisdiction, easily interpreted as the national territory. However, the national territory is quite limited if human rights must be respected. The Court therefore ruled that jurisdiction can equally be established when a State exercises control over a zone or territory, or when its agents exercise effective control over an individual.[86]

82 Article 19 (1) ECHR.

83 Article 19 (2) ECHR.

84 ECHR, *Affaire Hirsi Jamaa and others vs Italy*; (2012); Application No. 27765-/09, paras. 159–186.

85 ECHR *Soering v United Kingdom*; (1989) application No. 14038/88, para. 91.

86 ECHR, *Al Skeini v United Kingdom*; (2001) Application No. 55721/07, paras. 133–137 (authority and control of State Agents), points 138–140 (effective control in the zone).

1.2.4.3 *Human Rights in Other International and Regional Instruments*

The growing willingness to consider the extraterritorial application of human rights treaties when certain conditions are met, like the exercise of authority and effective control, is justified by the parallel increase of maritime law enforcement operations in wider expanses of the sea. Another judicial consideration in determining the extraterritorial application of a treaty is whether the treaty is self-executing, even if this aspect is not unique to maritime law enforcement or the maritime domain.[87]

Although UNCLOS does not expressly include the term 'human rights',[88] the application of human rights in the maritime environment has been judicially recognized for decades. The International Court of Justice partly held in 1949 that State obligations are 'based on certain general and well-based principles, namely: elementary considerations of humanity, even more exacting in peace than in war. …'[89] In 1999, and again in 2015, the International Tribunal for the Law of the Sea (ITLOS) declared that 'considerations of humanity must apply in the Law of the Sea as they do in other areas of international law.'[90]

A host of other conventions that do not have a primary focus on human rights include provisions that are either aspirational or expressly impose human rights-related obligations on State parties. A good example is the 2005 SUA Protocol which provides that where a State Party takes measures against a ship, it shall '[e]Ensure that all persons on board are treated in a manner which preserves their basic human dignity, and in compliance with the applicable provisions of international law, including international human

87 Carlos Manuel Vazquez, 'The Four Doctrines of Self-Executing Treaties' (1995) 89 AM. J .IN'L L. 695. The self-executing nature of a treaty is a matter of controversy and much confusion and 'at a general level, a self-executing treaty may be defined as a treaty that may be enforced in the courts without prior legislation by Congress, and a non-self-executing treaty may be defined as a treaty that may not be enforced without prior legislative implementation', *see ibid.* at 695.

88 See Bernard H. Oxman, 'Human Rights and the United Nations Convention on the Law of the Sea' (1997) 36 *Colum. J. Transit'* 399, 401: 'The United Nations Convention on the Law of the Sea is not ordinarily considered a human rights instrument. With a few exceptions, its role in advancing human rights is not obvious or direct. But neither is it negligible.'

89 The International Court of Justice addressed the right of innocent passage, loss of life, jurisdiction, and mining among other issues, and held in part, that State obligations 'are based … on certain general and well recognized principles, namely; elementary considerations of humanity, even more exacting in peace than in war', see *Corfu Channel (United Kingdom of Great Britain and Northern Ireland v. Albania)* 1949 I.C.J. 4, 22 (Apr.9).

90 The 'Enrica Lexie' Incident (Italy v. India), Case No. 24, Order of Aug. 24, 2015, 133, <https://www.itlos.org/en/main/cases/list-of-cases/case-no-24/> accessed 30 June 2023.

rights law ...[91] It should be stated that similar provisions are contained in the Terrorism Financing Convention and the Terrorist Bombings Convention.[92]

Furthermore, the Arms Trade Treaty (ATT), which entered into force on the 24th of December 2014, provides that a State Party, in the context of sanctioning the exportation of covered conventional arms, shall [a]Assess the potential that the conventional arms or items ... would contribute to undermine peace and security or could be used to ... commit or facilitate a serious violation of international human rights law.[93]

The State Party is then to take appropriate measures to regulate, where necessary and feasible, the transit or trans-shipment under its jurisdiction of conventional arms covered under Article 2(1) ATT through its territory in accordance with relevant international law. The ATT thus addresses human rights unequivocally by providing that even where an export is not proscribed, an exporting State Party shall assess the potential that the conventional arms or items could be used to commit or facilitate a serious violation of international human rights law.[94]

The application of human rights in activities carried out at sea can be further perceived in the fact that even instruments with no security focus make reference to the idea of humane treatment and humanity. Member States at the International Maritime Organization (IMO) amended SOLAS in 2004 to provide that '[m]asters of ships who have embarked persons in distress at sea shall treat them with humanity, within the capabilities and limitations of the ship.'[95]

Given the dense history of rulings that treat the intersection of human rights with maritime law enforcement operations in European venues, a close look at

---

91 *See* 2005 SUA Protocol, Article 8, 10.a.ii, 'Any person who is taken into custody, or regarding whom any other measures are taken or proceedings are being carried out pursuant to this Convention, shall be guaranteed fair treatment, including enjoyment of all rights and guarantees in conformity with the law of the State in the territory of which that person is present and applicable provisions of international law, including international human rights law.'

92 International Convention for the Suppression of the Financing of Terrorism Art 17, Dec. 9, 1999, 2178 U.N.T.S. 237; International Convention for the Suppression of Terrorist Bombings, Art 14, Dec. 15, 1997, S. Treaty Doc. No. 106-6, 2149 U.N.T.S. 256.

93 Article 7.1 United Nations Arms Trade Treaty (ATT), April 2, 2013, 52, I.L.M. 988.

94 Art. 7 1.b.ii, one ATT principle provides that State Parties respect 'human rights in accordance with, inter alia, the Charter of the United Nations and the Universal Declaration of Human Rights. ...'

95 International Maritime Organization MSC.153 (78), Amendments to the International Convention for the Safety of Life at Sea, MSC. 78/26/Add.1, Annex 3, Reg. 33.6 (May 20, 2004).

the ECtHR merits a little more attention. Besides numerous other things, the ECtHR may award 'just satisfaction and declare 'that certain actions, omissions, law or court decisions on the part of a State violate the Convention.'[96] The legal minds in Strasbourg are however not empowered to overrule or annul national laws, but can request the respective State to re-open the case along with granting a compensation award. Thus, the court provides 'open remedies', a term comprising a range of declaratory mechanisms by which courts communicate their conclusion that human rights have been violated but instead of devising an executory order or invalidating legislation, they invite other branches of government to decide how to address the identified human rights problem. The ECHR therefore plays the role of supreme arbiter in human rights protection in Europe as well as a supervisory court with a supporting and subsidiary role.

The prevailing legal and judicial landscape includes multiple conventions and court rulings which represent a broad and uneven terrain of authorities that impose multifarious human rights considerations in maritime law enforcement in drug trafficking, piracy, fisheries enforcement and most of all maritime migration.

1.3 *The Obligations under the International Law of the Sea*

Mishaps at sea are not new occurrences. The obligation of mariners to provide material aid in cases of distress encountered at sea has long been recognized in custom and tradition. A right to enter and remain in a safe harbour without prejudice, when obliged by the perils of the sea or *force majeure* is universally recognized. Such a right will however be incomplete if the victims in need of help are not assisted by actors who are available and capable of saving the situation. It is for this reason that the international law of the Sea enshrines the duty to provide assistance, duty to bring to a place of safety and the duty to provide a place for disembarkation.

1.3.1 The Duty to Provide Assistance

The duty to provide assistance to persons in danger of being lost at sea is unarguably one of the most well-established tenets of the law of the sea.[97] This tenet is succinctly enshrined in UNCLOS:

96 *See* Article 41 ECHR, 'If the court finds that there has been a violation of the Convention or the Protocols thereto, and if the internal law of the high contracting Party concerned allows only partial reparation to be made, the Court shall, if necessary, afford just satisfaction to the injured party.'

97 E. de Vattel, *Le Droit des gens ou principes de la loi naturelle; appliques a la conduit et aux affaires des nations et des souverains* Vol. 1 (1758) 170.

> Every State shall require the master of a ship flying its flag, in so far as he can do so without serious danger to the ship, the crew or the passengers;
> To render assistance to any person found at sea in danger of being lost;
> To proceed with all possible speed to the rescue of persons in distress, if informed of their need of assistance, in so far as such action may reasonably be expected of him[98]

Given the fact that this provision is not a self-executing norm, it is only logical to interpret that this duty is not the responsibility of individual mariners solely, but equally of the flag State of the mariner to ensure that an adequate transpositional law is enacted which imposes this obligation on the master of the ship.[99] A concrete example of such a transposition of Article 98(1) UNCLOS can be found in Germany where No. 2 of the Regulations concerning the safety of Seafaring in conjunction with No. 323c of the Criminal Code, envisages criminal sanctions for a failure to assist. Similarly, the duty to assist contained in the SOLAS Convention can neither be said to be self-executing.[100] The SOLAS Convention lays down as follows:

> Parties shall, as they are able to do so individually or in co-operation with other States and, as appropriate, with the Organization, participate in the development of search and rescue services to ensure that assistance is rendered to any person in distress at sea. On receiving information that any person is, or appears to be, in distress at sea, the responsible authorities of a party shall take urgent steps to ensure that the necessary assistance is provided[101]

It should be noted here that the scope of the duty *rationae personae* is broadly formulated to the benefit of' any person' in UNCLOS and regardless of ... the circumstances in which that person is found'. This relevance of this formulation becomes apparent when considering the fact that many of the persons in need of assistance are 'economic refugees'. Besides the actual fact of finding a person at sea, the sole material requirement necessary to bring about the duty to provide assistance is the existence of a situation of distress on board, a term defined in the SAR Convention as a 'situation wherein there is a reasonable

98 Article 98 (1) UNCLOS.

99 A. Proelss, 'Rescue at sea Revisited; What Obligations Exist towards Refugees?' (2008) *Scandinavian Institute of Maritime Law Yearbook* 10.

100 Annex, chapter V, reg. 10 (a) SOLAS; and Annex, chapter 2, para. 2.1.10 SAR: 'Parties shall ensure that assistance be provided to any person in distress at sea'.

101 Annex, chapter 2, para. 2.1.10 SAR.

certainty that a vessel or a person is threatened by grave and imminent danger and requires immediate assistance'.[102] Despite the apparent clarity of the preceding provisions, the full extent of the duty to render assistance or, more precisely, the existence and scope of related duties such as bringing the persons to a place of safety and many others, require greater clarification.

1.3.2 Bring to a Place of Safety

Prior to examining the prickly issue of disembarkation, it is pivotal to state that despite contradictory scholarly opinion, the flag State is obliged to bring rescued persons to a place of safety. This obligation is a logical consequence of the definition of rescue contained in the SAR Convention: 'RESCUE. An operation to retrieve persons in distress, provide for their initial medical or other needs, and deliver them to a place of safety.'[103]

Given the yawning absence of any specific definition of what can be considered a *place of safety*, regular and common practice has imposed an interpretation that favours the 'next port of call' of the ship as 'the place of safety'.[104] This approach comfortably relies on the opinions expressed by the Executive Committee (EXCOM) of the UNHCR.[105] The EXCOM promotes the advantages of a practical solution to the problems connected with the rescue of asylum seekers and thus, with respect to the rescue of persons on the high seas, it is safe to assume that in numerous occasions, the nearest port in terms of geographical proximity will generally be the next port of call considering the overriding safety concerns involved.[106] In the same light, the European Commission has stated that 'obligations relating to search and rescue include the transport to a safe place'.[107]

Despite the lack of fluidity in the analysis, the duty of the flag State to bring rescuees to a place of safety cannot be placed on equal terms with the duty

102 Annex, chapter 1, para. 1.3.11 SAR.

103 Annex, chapter 1, para. 1.3.2 SAR. Despite the non-obligatory nature of this provision, it is indicative of the understanding shared by the States Parties to the SAR Convention as to what a rescue actually entails.

104 It should be noted that this interpretation has no reliable legal backing, *see* Richard Barnes, 'Refugee Law at Sea' (2004) 53(1) *International and Comparative Law Quarterly* 47, 51.

105 UNHCR, Conclusions adopted by the Executive Committee on the international Protection of Refugees, 1975–2009, No. 23 (XXXII) 31 <https://www.unhcr.org/media/conclusions-adopted-executive-committee-international-protection-refugees-1975-2009> accessed 30 June 2023.

106 EXCOM, No. 26 (XXXIII) 34.

107 Commission Staff Working Document, Study on the International law instruments in relation to illegal immigration by sea, SEC (2007) 691, 15 May 2007, para. 2.3.2, referencing the duty contained in the SAR Convention.

to disembark. It is neither odd nor out of place for a ship to be considered as a place of safety or, alternatively, it may enter a place of safety where the persons on board may receive whatever provisions of medical attention deemed necessary without obligatorily disembarking from the ship. The IMO Maritime Safety Committee however states that even in situations where the ship is capable of safely accommodating the survivors, and may serve as a temporary place of safety, it should be relieved of this duty as soon as alternative arrangements can be made.[108] With this in mind, greater light needs to be shed on whether the flag State is obliged to disembark and whether the coastal State is obliged to accept disembarkations.

1.3.3 Duty to Allow for Disembarkation

For a very long time, disembarkation, which constitutes the last phase of rescue operations, has been a focal point of discord. This stems from the fact that rescue operations imply that the assisted people should be delivered 'to a place of safety'.[109] Even if a ship can be considered as temporal place of safety, the rescued people will eventually need to be disembarked on dry land.[110] Logically, disembarkation could happen in the next port of call of the rescuing ship, on the land closest to the place of rescue, at a place indicated by those rescued or at any other place where assistance can be comfortably given. This hypothetical situation is far from the reality where it is very difficult to find a State that will permit the disembarkation of rescued people in its ports by a rescue vessel, especially when there is a likelihood of applications for asylum within the receiving State.

In general, disembarkation is subject to the principle of sovereignty, which requires permission from the receiving State before a vessel can use its ports, and the principle of non-refoulement, which prohibits the return of rescued people back to where their lives are endangered or where they can be subjected to degrading and inhumane treatment as was initially envisaged for

108 International Maritime Organization (IMO), Resolution MSC.167 (78), Guidelines on the Treatment of Persons Rescued At Sea (20 May 2004) annex 34, no. 6.13 <https://www.refworld.org/docid/432acb464.html> accessed 30 June 2023.

109 Section 1.3.2 SAR.

110 According to Resolution 167(78) of the IMO Rescue Guidelines, *supra* note 33, a 'place of safety' is 'allocation where rescue operations are considered to terminate. It is also a place where the survivors' safety of life is no longer threatened and where their basic human needs (such as food, shelter and medical needs) can be met. Further, it is a place from which transportation arrangements can be made for the survivors' next or final destination.'

refugees.[111] Nowadays, the principle is applicable to any person who might suffer a violation of his or her right to life or freedom from torture.[112]

Most often, the rescue operations are followed by disputes as to which State ought to receive the rescuing vessel and which State should accept the rescued people. This has been very recurrent in recent years in cases of assistance to migrants by sea since States are often reluctant to rescue irregular migrants and asylum seekers, even electing to shut their ports to rescuing vessels as was the case with the Tampa[113] or the more recent German Captain Rackete treated below.

Faced with the above uncertainty, resort can be made in the 2004 amended SAR Convention that tries to attribute the obligations by stating that:

> Parties shall co-ordinate and co-operate to ensure that masters of ships providing assistance by embarking persons in distress at sea are released from their obligations with minimum further deviation from the ships' intended voyage, provided that releasing the master of the ship from the obligations does not further endanger the safety of life at sea. The Party responsible for the search and rescue region in which such assistance is rendered shall exercise primary responsibility for ensuring such co-ordination and co-operation occurs, so that survivors assisted are disembarked from the assisting ship and delivered to a place of safety, taking into account the particular circumstances of the case and guidelines developed by the (Inter-Governmental Maritime Consultative) Organization. In these cases, the relevant Parties shall arrange for such disembarkation to be effective as soon as reasonably practicable.[114]

A focused study of the above text unfortunately fails to resolve the issue of identifying the State responsible for disembarking the rescued people. The provision only assumes that States will coordinate and that primary responsibility will be limited to ensuring that such coordination and cooperation materializes. The text refrains from clearly identifying the State responsible for

111 Article 33 of the 1951 Convention on the Status of Refugees, 189 UNTS 137, 28 July 1951 (entered into force 22 April 1954).

112 European Court of Human Rights (ECtHR), *Chahal v. The United Kingdom*, Application No. 22414/93, Judgment (Grand Chamber), 15 November 1996, para. 74; and ECtHR, *Hirsi Jamaa and Other v. Italy*, Application No. 27765/09, Judgment (Grand Chamber), 23 February 2012, para. 114.

113 Cecilia Baillet, 'The Tampa Case and Its Impact on Burden Sharing at Sea' (2003) 25(3) *Human Rights Quarterly* 759.

114 Chapter 3.1.9 SAR; similar text was inserted in the revised Regulation 4.1.1 SOLAS.

disembarkation and the action to be taken in the absence of an agreement to cooperate. The solution to this dilemma therefore must be sought from other sources.

The dilemma of deciding whether there is an obligation to allow for disembarkation of rescued persons at a place of safety revolves around the interests of the flag State on the one hand, and the interests of the coastal State on the other. However, given that disembarkation involves entering the territorial or even the internal waters of the State, complex issues of territorial sovereignty tend to arise. This dilemma has been aptly diagnosed by scholars to be a major source of the ineffectiveness of implementing the duty to allow for disembarkation. One scholar points out that any obligation of a flag State to disembark shipwrecked persons at the next port of call will turn out to be useless, were it not logically linked with the corresponding duty of the coastal State of the next port of call to temporarily accept rescued persons on its territory.[115]

It is therefore imperative to ascertain the duty of the flag State to disembark rescuees. This duty will unavoidably be linked with the right to enter the territory of the coastal State. Such a duty would no doubt constitute an infringement on the territorial sovereignty of the State in question that is unimaginable. Although a miniscule number of bold scholars opine against this state of affairs, no relevant international conventions provide for such an obligation. The argument for an obligation to disembark holds that:

> Given that there is a duty to provide assistance at sea, any act which will undermine the carrying out of such rescue is tantamount to a breach of international law. An absolute refusal to accept disembarkation limits the possibility or likelihood of rescue taking place and thus it could be seen as undermining the execution of the rescue in the first place. Consequently, a right to disembarkation on the part of the rescues must exist along with the corresponding duty on the flag and coastal States to carry out and respect the disembarkation respectively.[116]

Futile arguments have been made to ground this duty on paragraph 1.3.2 of the SAR Convention, claiming that the provision is indicative of more than an implicit obligation to deliver to a place of safety. Such attempts are quashed with the simple motivation that the particular provision is merely a definition without any distinct obligatory content thus rendering the argument

115 Proelss, *supra* note 69, 14–15.
116 UNHCR, *supra* note 75, Annex 1, para. 9.

erroneous.[117] More recent literature opines that the actual obligatory norm simply requires that, rather than rescue, 'assistance be provided to any person in distress at sea',[118] thus dodging the incorporation of an explicit duty on the flag State to disembark, into the SAR Convention.[119]

Despite the absence of an explicit duty to disembark, it is still possible to infer such a duty. One such inference can be seen with an in-depth examination of the notion of 'rescue' as a single unified act that starts with the physical act of removing persons from the waters or from a vessel in distress and extending until the point in time at which such persons have entered a place of safety and disembarked the rescuing ship. This approach tallies squarely with the practical approach advocated by the UNHCR EXCOM by uplifting the primary responsibility of the ship master within a very short period.[120] Most importantly, it satisfies the humanitarian purpose and intention of Article 98 (1) UNCLOS, alongside the relevant norms of the SAR and SOLAS Conventions. This is based on a wide comprehension of the requirement of 'place of safety' that cannot be considered to have been adequately met if the rescued persons are to be indefinitely maintained on board the rescuing vessel. This approach however fails to integrate the non-obligatory nature of the term used with respect to 'rescue' and the penchant shown for the term 'assistance'.

The other argument is based on recent trends that show a presumption in favour of disembarkation, obliging coastal States *prima facie* to accept the disembarkation of persons rescued at sea unless there are tangible reasons to suspect a disturbance of public order. The declarations made by the MSC of the IMO after the 2004 amendments to the SOLAS and SAR Conventions seem to defend this increasingly popular trend that favours the presumption of disembarkation. Their pronouncements are particularly visible where the contracting parties are enjoined to 'arrange disembarkation as soon as reasonably practicable'.[121] The UNHCR Working Group on the Question of Rescue of Asylum Seekers at Sea further buttresses this stance by stating that

117 This provision is found in the section of SAR entitled 'Terms and Definitions'. Logically, it cannot generate norms of an obligatory character.

118 Annex, chapter 2, para. 2.1.10 SAR.

119 Proelss, *supra* note 69, 16.

120 UNHCR, EXCOM docs, No. 26 (XXXIII), 34.

121 Inter-Agency, 'Rescue at Sea. A Guide to Principles and Practice as Applied to Migrants and Refugees' (Sept 2006), <https://www.refworld.org/docid/45b8d1e54.html> accessed 30 June 2023.

'asylum seekers rescued at sea should normally be disembarked at the next port of call'.[122]

However enticing these declarations may sound, the timorous choice of the term 'should' immediately weakens the applicability. More so, treaty law does not support this presumption in any way despite the discretion this presumption would grant to coastal States to either deny or grant permission to disembark. It can therefore be concluded that despite the existence of a duty on the flag States to assist those in need and on the coastal States to ensure the existence of mechanisms to ensure the rapid provision of assistance, there is no duty on the flag State to disembark the rescued persons, nor is there an adjacent duty on the coastal State under the terms of the international law of the sea to accept any disembarkations.

The disembarkation dilemma constitutes a serious protection problem for migrants rescued at sea[123] by exposing them to serious risks of harm, ranging from refoulement to violence or mistreatment on board a vessel. States that actually permit disembarkation are under no clear obligation to allow entry or conduct an initial screening to distinguish those requiring international protection. Yet another risk is that those in distress would simply be abandoned at sea by vessels unwilling to risk the costly burden of being unable to disembark those it rescues. Even heart-rending is the observation that this morbid trend is on the rise.[124]

122 UNHCR, Preliminary Report on Suggestions Retained by the Working Group of Government Representatives on the Question of Rescue of Asylum-Seekers at Sea, 1 October 1982, EC/SCP/24, http://www.unhcr.org/refworld/docid/45b8d1e54.html> accessed 30 June 2023.

123 Richard Barnes, 'Refugee Law at Sea' (2004) 53(1) *International and Comparative Law Quarterly* 47 examining legal obligations existing upon coastal States and flag States in respect to asylum seekers rescued at sea.

124 *See* UNHCR, Summary of Discussions and Recommendations, Expert Meeting on Interception and Rescue in the Mediterranean, Cooperative Responses, Sept. 12–13, 2005, Athens (citing among the possible consequences of the disembarkation problem the risk of refusal by shipmasters to respond to distress calls, and the possibility of rescued persons being thrown overboard or encouraged to swim ashore.). In 2005, Vincent Cochetel, Deputy Director of UNHCR's Department of International Protection, observed that disembarkation refusal could have serious consequences on the rescue regime itself when he observed that, '[t]he next time (captains) see a ship at sea they will turn a blind eye, not answer a distress call, or throw (the migrants) overboard' *see Ship Owners Facing 'Unfair' Migrant Rescue Burden, Says UN Refugee Section*, UNHCR News Archives, 14 September 2005.

1.4 *The Obligations Incumbent on Flag and Coastal States*

Given the high tendency of maritime actors to constantly ignore their duties or attribute it to others, it was pivotal to clearly identify and codify the maritime actors who should be held liable for any unfortunate event resulting from the failure to render assistance, to search and rescue and the failure to comply with obligations which were expressly within the capacity of the flag State or the coastal State.

1.4.1 The Duty to Render Assistance

The duty to render assistance at sea is enshrined in Article 98-(1) UNCLOS thus:

1. Every State shall require the master of a ship flying its flag, in so far as he can do so without serious danger to the ship, the crew or the passengers;
   a) To render assistance to any person found at sea in danger of being lost;
   b) To proceed with all possible speed to the rescue of persons in distress, if informed of their need of assistance, in so far as such action may reasonably be expected of him;
   c) After a collision, to render assistance to the other ship, its crew and its passengers and, where possible, to inform the other ship of the name of its own ship, its port of registry and the nearest port at which it will call …

It is worth noting that prior to the adoption of UNCLOS, two other international treaties had codified the duty to render assistance, namely the 1974 International Convention for the Safety of Life at Sea (SOLAS)[125] and the 1979 International Convention on Maritime Search and Rescue (SAR). The latter came to light due to repeated instances of non-rescue at sea during the Indo-Chinese refugee crisis in the mid-1970s[126] and sought to identify those responsible for rescue operations and the consequences of their actions. As a result of its repetition in treaty and domestic law, mindful of State practice, despite the

125 1184 United Nations Treaty Series, No 1861 (SOLAS).

126 As a consequence of the growing number of refugees coming from the former Indochina, the neighbouring countries which were receiving refugees in the region decided to close their borders and ban any further disembarkation; *see* UNHCR, Consultative meeting, Geneva, December 1978, HC Statements, December 1978.

lack of uniformity,[127] the duty to render assistance is recognised as a principle of customary law.[128]

The SAR Convention strives to create an international system of coordinating rescue operations that guarantees their effectiveness and safety. State Parties are thus invited to conclude SAR agreements with neighbouring States to regulate and coordinate SAR operations and services within an agreed maritime zone. Such agreements are designed to technically comply and render operational, the obligations provided in Article 98-(2) UNCLOS, which stipulates that:

> Every coastal State shall promote the establishment, operation and maintenance of an adequate and effective search and rescue service regarding safety on and over the sea and, where circumstances so require, by way of mutual agreements cooperate with neighbouring States for this purpose.

Such agreements equally reduce the risk of non-rescue incidents and constitute a commercial boon for the contracting parties who carry out SAR operations.

It is fundamental to note that the execution of rescue operations does not exhaust the duty to render assistance, which extends to the disembarkation of the rescued persons in a place of safety. The MSC of the IMO amended both the SAR and SOLAS conventions. Consequently, pursuit to Article 4.1 of Chapter V/33 of the SOLAS Convention and Chapter 3.1.9 of the Annex to the SAR Convention, the coastal State responsible for the search and rescue in the region in which the SAR operation took place shall exercise 'primary responsibility' for ensuring such coordination and cooperation occurs, so that the 'survivors assisted are disembarked' from the assisting ship and delivered to 'a place of safety'.[129] As per the MSC Guidelines,[130] a 'place of safety' is a location where the rescue operations are considered complete. In this light, Principles 6.13 and 6.14 of the Guidelines opine that the rescue unit can be the place of safety, but

127 The interpretation of the obligation is still subject to wide controversy. There is a lack of consensus on the obligations of the coastal States in whose zones the rescue operations take place and on the place where the rescued persons can disembark, *see* 13 Feb 2009, FS117/15/1 IMO.

128 UN Commission on International Law, 'Commentary on Draft Article 12 of the United Nations Convention on the High Seas' (1956) UN Doc.A/3179.

129 V/gg, art 4.1-1 SOLAS and N.8, Annex, c.3.1.9 SAR.

130 IMO, 'Guidelines on the Treatment of Persons Rescued at Sea' (May 2004) MSC.167 (78), <https://www.refworld.org/docid/432acb464.html> accessed 30 June 2023. These Guidelines are not binding for the States Parties to the 2004 Amendments, but rather recommendations on the interpretation and application of the amended text.

only provisionally. In fact, the text lays emphasis on the roles of the flag and coastal States in replacing the master of the rescuing vessel.

Moreover, pursuant to the MSC Guidelines, the State in whose SAR zone the operation took place has the duty to provide or at least secure, a place of safety for the rescue persons (Principle 2-5). This principle does not include a right of entry into the territory of this State by the rescued persons or a right of access to the ports of the coastal State. It simply requires the coastal State to carry out the SAR operation from start to finish. By implication, the rescued persons are not to be left at sea whatever their status.[131]

Mindful of the non-binding nature of the MSC Guidelines, Principle 2.5 suggests that coastal States have a 'residual obligation' of allowing disembarkation on its own territory if it is impossible to do so anywhere else. This position was further clarified by the IMO Facilitation Committee (FAL), which adopted the 'Principles relating to administrative procedures for disembarking persons rescued at sea'[132] in January 2009. Principle 3 prescribes as follows:

> If disembarkation from the rescuing ship cannot be arranged swiftly elsewhere, the Government responsible for the SAR area should accept the disembarkation of the persons rescued in accordance with immigration laws and regulations of each member State into a place of safety under its control in which the persons rescued can have timely access to post-rescue support.

The obligatory intervention of the FAL is a clear indication that the SAR and SOLAS Conventions were glaringly inadequate to properly enhance the safety of persons rescued at sea. The MSC Guidelines and the FAL clearly prescribe how these amendments should be implemented although the suggestions are yet to be considered in practice. Besides, the obligations of coastal States and numerous other issues are still pending consensus. A crystal example is the diffuse situation of the obligations of international organizations which carry out maritime activities alongside States. This situation arises because the above provisions make exclusive reference to the flag and coastal States. In practice,

131 The issue concerning the denial of disembarkation by coastal States was raised in situations where irregular migrants and asylum seekers were among the rescued persons, *see* A. Fischer-Lescano, T. Lohrand, T. Tohidipur, 'Border controls at sea; Requirements under international human rights and refugee law' (2009) 21(2) International Journal of Refugee Law 256–296.

132 IMO, Principles Relating to Administrative Procedures for Disembarking Persons Rescued at Sea, FAL 3/Circ. 194, 22, January 2009 <https://www.refworld.org/docid/524be8244.html> accessed 30 June 2023.

there are numerous police activities performed under the command of international organizations or supra-national bodies.[133] Whether or not such entities ought to comply with the duty to render assistance requires clarification. In fact, their duty to render assistance may only be activated under customary international law if the scope is extended to a *rationae personae* application, or if new texts or amendments to the existing instruments are adopted in order to include such entities.

A separate issue is the identification of the beneficiaries of the assistance. Whether it is a purely inter-state issue or individual rights can be claimed in this respect merits attention. It should be noted that the international law of the sea does not consider the private sector or individuals as its main focus. Thus, the international law of the sea simply attributes rights and obligations in the different maritime zones among States. However, the rapid increase in activities at sea and the corresponding increase in human presence raise the question of the legal framework applicable to the human element, particularly the application of human rights at sea. Contemporary academic research opines that the law of the sea, specifically UNCLOS, should progressively embrace community interests, especially the protection of human rights, stressing the complementarity of these two sets of international law. With this scholarship as foundation, the duty to render assistance can be considered as the operational obligation derived from the application of human right of life.

1.4.2 Search and Rescue

The duty to rescue persons in distress is one of the most ancient and fundamental principles of the law of the sea.[134] Thanks to its vastly established nature as a conventional rule, it can comfortably be seen as an integral part of customary international law. However, as clearly examined above, its silence on the disembarkation of rescued persons makes it quite incomplete. As a consequence, coastal States are more inclined to welcome those less in need of refuge than those most in need of refuge given the potential burden it poses. It therefore appears logical to peruse this obligation from the viewpoint of the flag State on the one hand, and from the coastal State on the other hand.

133 Operations carried out by the European Border and Coastguard Agency (FRONTEX), <https://frontex.europa.eu/what-we-do/operations/operations/> accessed 30 June 2023.

134 De Vattel of the 18th century acknowledged the special humanitarian consideration owed to vessels in distress. E de Vattel, '*The Law of Nations*' (J. Chitty, Trans- London 1834) 170.

1.4.3 Obligations of Flag State

As enshrined in Article 98(1) UNCLOS:

> Every State shall require the master of a ship flying its flag, in so far as he can do so without serious danger to the ship, the crew, or the passengers ... to render assistance to any person found in danger of being lost ... and to proceed with all possible speed to the rescue of persons in distress, if informed of their need for assistance, in so far as such action may be reasonably expected of him.

In the same vein, as provided in the SOLAS Convention:

> The master of a ship at sea which is in a position to be able to provide assistance, on receiving a signal from any source that persons are in distress at sea, is bound to proceed with all speed to their assistance, if possible informing them or the search and rescue service, that the ship is doing so. If the ship receiving the distress alert is unable or, in the special circumstances of the case, considers it unreasonable or unnecessary to proceed to their assistance, the master must enter in the log-book the reason for failing to proceed to the assistance of the persons in distress and, taking into account the recommendations of the Organization, inform the appropriate search and rescue services accordingly.[135]

Though States are held by this obligation, it is predominantly carried out by mariners in practice. In fact, States are enjoined to incorporate this provision into their domestic laws.[136] Furthermore, the obligation to rescue persons in distress at sea carries no exception and no discrimination may be made according to the legal status of the persons to be rescued. The Brussels Salvage Convention provides to this effect that 'the duty to assist applies to everybody, even though an enemy, found at sea in danger of being lost'.[137] The SAR Convention further buttresses this aspect by requiring that 'assistance is to be provided regardless of the nationality or status of the persons to be rescued

135 Chapter V, Reg 10(a) SOLAS.

136 The UK imposes this duty on the master of a vessel, upon receiving a distress signal, to proceed to their assistance unless unable, or in the circumstances, it would be unreasonable or unnecessary to do so. Failure to do so will constitute a criminal offence, *see* Section 93 (1) and (2) of the Merchant Shipping Act of 1995.

137 Article 11. Brussels Salvage Convention.

or the circumstances in which that person was found'.[138] Even international organizations have enjoined flag States to ensure that masters observe the duty to rescue persons in distress at sea.[139]

Despite the unambiguous nature of this rule and the impressive international legal arsenal accompanying it, it is distressing to observe its quasi-absence in domestic legislations thus explaining its feeble application. With the practical challenges encountered in the enforcement of this obligation, there is a high likelihood of violations without any legal consequences. Furthermore, in most cases, the flag State is best placed to enforce the obligation to assist those in distress. Considering the disturbing observation that most sea-faring vessels are actually registered under flags of convenience in States that are unlikely to supervise the enforcement of this obligation, the doomed position of persons in distress at sea becomes even more evident.[140] In addition, mammoth disincentives to providing assistance exist, especially where such assistance could orchestrate delays in deliveries.[141]

In a nutshell, this obligation engages numerous loopholes such as tenuous enforcement, unclear ambits of the rescue operation and many others. The compelling moral justifications are ably challenged by equally compelling commercial demands, regardless of the notion that no reason can be evoked for denying assistance.[142] Even the precision of international legal instruments

138 Article 2.1.10 SAR.

139 Report of the 28th Session of the Executive Committee, A/AC.86/549, paras. 21–36 B (d). *See also* EXCOM Conclusions No 23 (XXXII) 1981 and No 38 (XXXVIO 1985; INO Resolution 920 (22) 2001.

140 Oxman and Coombs note that in practice no one expects Liberia, a flag of convenience State, to extradite, try and punish those committing crimes on board vessels flying their flag, see BH Oxman and M Coombs, 'Jurisdiction-Constitutionality of the U.S. State's Jurisdiction Over Criminal Acts Occurring on the High Seas-Consistency of Such Jurisdiction with International Law-Effects Doctrine' (2001) 95 *American Journal of International Law* 438, 442.

141 The *Tampa* was covered by Assuranceforingen Gard. Rule 32 of the cover provides that: 'The Association shall cover costs and expenses reasonably incurred in consequence of the Ship having stowaways, refugees or persons saved at sea on board, but only to the extent that the Member is legally liable for the costs and expenses or they are incurred with the approval of the Association. The cover does not include consequential loss of profit or depreciation', <http://www.gard.no/Publications/statutesandrules/rules/p2-chapter.html> accessed 1 December 2002.

142 Under the common law, commercial considerations are no reason for failing to respond to a distress call. See *Scaramanga v Stamp.* [1880] 5 CPD 295. It is notable that although vessels assisting people in distress may be severely inconvenienced, they are protected against loss insurance policies, which specifically provides for cover to reimburse vessel owners against such losses. However, insurance cover is often inadequate in this respect.

like the SAR Convention[143] and the International Aeronautical and Maritime Search and Rescue Manual[144] do not resolve the issue of the extent of this duty. Common maritime practice therefore limits itself to the disembarkation of persons at the next port of call, given the commercial advantages, despite the absence of any definite rule to this effect. Consequently, the popular interpretation trend, notwithstanding its unsatisfactory outcome, is to conclude that bringing distressed persons on board or transferring them to another vessel amounts to delivery at a place of safety.

1.4.4 Obligations of the Coastal State

According to the SOLAS Convention, chapter V, regulation 15(a):

> Each contracting Government undertakes to ensure that any necessary arrangements are made for coast watching and for the rescue of persons in distress at sea round its coasts. These arrangements should include the establishment, operation and maintenance of such maritime safety facilities as are deemed practicable and necessary having regard to the density of the sea going traffic and the navigational dangers and should, so far as possible, afford adequate means of locating and rescuing such persons.[145]

In a similar posture, UNCLOS obliges coastal States to provide rescue and assistance in the Exclusive Economic Zone and in the high seas.[146] Strangely though, the same convention makes no mention of such an obligation with respect to the territorial sea. It may however not be considered ultra vires to consider this vacuum as implicit in the provisions on innocent passage.[147] The SAR convention on the other hand is more eloquent on the specific obligations by clearly stating that:

143 Para 1.3.2 SAR, 'Operation to retrieve persons in distress, provide for their initial medical or other needs, and deliver them to a place of safety'.

144 Vol. III, s.2 International Aeronautical and Maritime Search and Rescue Manual, 'Must be delivered to a place of safety as quickly as possible'.

145 The present provision is now contained in Regulation V-7(3) SOLAS.

146 Articles 58(2) and 86 UNCLOS.

147 Oxman denies that the coastal State could somehow rely on its sovereign authority in the territorial sea to exclude itself from any search and rescue obligations, arguing that preclude emergency rescue is a perverse insult to any rational concept of territorial sovereignty at sea, *see* B.H. Oxman, 'Human Rights and the United Nations Convention on the Law of the Sea' (1997) 36 *Columbia Journal of Transnational Law* 399, 414.

> Parties shall, as they are able to do so individually or in co-operation with other States and, as appropriate, with the Organization, participate in the development of search and rescue services to ensure that assistance is rendered to any person in distress at sea. On receiving information that any person is, or appears to be, in distress at sea, the responsible authorities of a party shall take urgent steps to ensure that the necessary assistance is provided.[148]

Again, '[p]arties shall ensure that assistance be provided to any person in distress at sea. They shall do so regardless of the nationality of status of such a person or the circumstances in which that person is found'.[149]

It is equally pivotal to determine the exact duration, scope or ambits of the rescue operation. As succinctly laid down by Article 1.3.2 SOLAS, a rescue operation constitutes 'an operation to retrieve persons in distress, provide for initial medical or other needs, and deliver them to a place of safety'. This clarity cannot however be comfortably construed as an obligation to allow the rescued persons to disembark to the coastal State. With this uncertainty, paragraph 3.1.2 provides a subtle orientation by stating that:

> Unless otherwise agreed between the States concerned, a Party should authorize, subject to applicable national laws, rules and regulations, immediate entry into or over its territory of rescue units of other Parties solely for the purpose of searching for the position of maritime casualties and rescuing the survivors of such casualties. In such cases, search and rescue operations shall, as far as practicable, be coordinated by the appropriate rescue co-ordination center of the Party which has authorized entry, or such other authority as has been designated by that Party.

Despite this encouraging language, the obligation is subjected to 'applicable national law, rules and regulations' thereby weakening the implementation of this obligation that can be argued to only arise when enshrined in a law, rule of regulation and not as a matter of policy. A subjective interpretation can be abused to the detriment of distressed persons at sea. To this effect, the SAR Convention states, in relation to the carrying out of coordinated rescue operations based on reliable information 'that a search and rescue operation has been successful, or that the emergency no longer exists, it shall terminate the

148 Para 2.1.1 SAR.

149 Para 2.1.10 SAR.

search and rescue operation and promptly so inform in authority, facility or service which has been notified'.[150]

Thus, the extent of a rescue operation must be a question of fact that can be objectively determined. The duration of the rescue must be in phase with the safety of the persons in distress. Where the concerned persons remain in difficulty and are still in need of essential human requirements like food, water and shelter, it will be wrong to claim that the search and rescue operation has ended.[151]

The search and rescue operations under SOLAS, UNCLOS and SAR are not self-executing. This justifies the reluctance of coastal States to facilitate rescue operations and receive asylum seekers. There is therefore an unparalleled need for greater cooperation by coastal States in rescue operations, greater certainty as regards the extent of the obligation to assist those in distress and a more attentive implementation of such international obligations in domestic law. Mindful of these considerations, the main challenge remains the wide discretion enjoyed by coastal States in determining the extent of search and rescue operations.

1.5 *Right of Passage and Refuge*

There is a clear-cut distinction between the rights of passage and rights of entry into sea ports. Most often, rescued persons in vessels may wish to avail themselves of these rights separately. In addition, the weight of human rights obligations on coastal States may have far reaching implications in respect to their territorial sea, internal waters and the rights to traverse such waters. Protecting rescued migrants at sea can be more efficient if these two rights are examined piecemeal.

1.5.1 Rights of Passage

Articles 2 and 3 UNCLOS designates 12-miles of territorial sea in which the coastal State can exercise sovereignty. The right of innocent passage stipulates that a vessel may navigate the territorial sea without entering the internal waters, and includes the right to proceed to and from port facilities and roadsteads.[152] The same Article 18 UNCLOS further insists that such passage must be 'continuous and expeditious' except for stopping or anchoring 'incidental to ordinary navigation or rendered necessary by force majeure or

150 Para 4.8.3 SAR.

151 See M. Davies, *compare* M White, 'MV Tampa Incident and Australia's Obligations' (2007) 122 *Maritime Studies* 7, 10.

152 Article 18 UNCLOS.

distress or for the purpose of rendering assistance to persons, ships or aircraft in danger or distress'. The paramount value of this right is however enshrined in Article 24 UNCLOS stating that:

> The coastal State shall not hamper the innocent passage of foreign ships through the territorial sea except in accordance with this convention or of any laws or regulations adopted in conformity with this Convention, the coastal State shall not:
>
> a) Impose requirements on foreign ships which have the practical effect of denying or impairing the right of innocent passage; or
>
> b) Discriminate in any form or in fact against the ships of any State or against ships carrying cargoes to or from or on behalf of any State.[153]

Under Article 19(1) UNCLOS, passage is not innocent if it is prejudicial to the 'peace, good order or security of the coastal State'. Article 19(2) goes on to list the activities which are considered prejudicial. However, more relevant to this reflection is the content of Article 19(2) (g) which stipulates prohibits the 'loading or unloading of any commodity, currency or person contrary to the customs, fiscal, immigration or sanitary laws and regulations of the coastal State'.[154]

It is equally important to state that UNCLOS requires coastal States to give due publicity to any such laws and regulations affecting passage.[155] The reason for such publicity is to ensure that vessels have adequate knowledge of local laws that could render innocent passage criminal or non-innocent. Failing to publicize such laws yet applying them on vessels seeking innocent passage can be seen as prejudging the activities of such vessels without due legal process thus violating the provisions of the refugee convention.[156]

It is theoretically possible to distinguish between vessels commencing a voyage with the principal intention of transporting illegal migrants from vessels stopping to assist those in distress. The former should be treated by legal proceedings while the latter deserves the cooperation of the involved parties. It is however practically onerous to effect such a distinction and innocent migrants meritorious of reception can suffer the consequences leading to an erosion of their asylum rights. Article 19(2) UNCLOS is no doubt not exhaustive

153 Article 24(1) UNCLOS.

154 Article 21(1)(h) UNCLOS provides that coastal States with the corresponding authority to enact laws to prevent the infringement of customs, fiscal, immigrations or sanitary laws, and regulations of the coastal State.

155 Article 21(3) UNCLOS.

156 Article 38(2) UNCLOS.

and the coastal State retains the right to determine threats to its security in the spirit of the Convention.

Even where the passage is innocent, temporary suspension is still possible within the framework of Article 25(3) UNCLOS:

> The coastal State may, without discrimination in form or in fact among foreign ships, suspend temporarily in specified areas of its territorial sea the innocent passage of foreign ships if such suspension is essential for the protection of its security, including weapons exercises. Such suspensions shall take effect only after having been duly published.

In essence, the conditions for such a temporary suspension include the fact that they must be non-discriminatory and must be published. However, the exact meaning of publicity is not defined and left to the discretion of the coastal State.

Where passage is not innocent, the coastal State may take necessary steps to prevent passage in its territorial sea.[157] It is therefore safe to say that the coastal State exercises sovereignty over the territorial sea subject to certain restrictions. Where these restrictions are either absent, dormant, or ambiguous, the presumption must be that the coastal State has the authority to act.[158]

1.5.2 Entry into Sea Ports and Rights of Refuge

Ports are of course located within internal waters thus fall under the regime of sovereignty of the coastal State.[159] Innocent passage however is not synonymous to a right of entry into port. In fact, even the presumption that ports are open for commerce cannot be construed a right.[160] If such a right is not expressly provided for by a treaty, the right remains a privilege. It should be immediately stated that neither the Convention on the Territorial Sea and

157 Article 25(1) UNCLOS.

158 'International law permits freedom of action for States, unless there is a rule constraining this'. M Shaw, *International Law* (4th edition Cambridge Grotius Press 1997) 150; and judgment of the Permanent Court of International Justice, The Case of the S.S. "Lotus" (France v. Turkey) (1928) PCIJ Series A, No, 18.

159 In the Nicaragua case, the ICJ confirmed that internal waters are subject to the sovereignty of the State and that it is 'by virtue of its sovereignty that the coastal State may regulate access to its ports', *Military and Paramilitary Activities in and against Nicaragua (Nicaragua v. United States of America). Merits*, Judgment. I.C.J. Reports 1986, p. 14, at paras. 212–13.

160 A.V. Lowe, 'The Right of Entry into Maritime Ports in International Law' (1977) 14 *San Diego Law Review* 597, 619.

Contiguous Zone[161] nor UNCLOS establish a right of entry into foreign ports. The Maritime Ports Convention of 1923 only evokes the need for reciprocity in the application of rights of access to, and equality of treatment within ports.[162] However, given the extremely low popularity of the Maritime Ports Convention in terms of ratification, resort is often made to customary international law.[163] Coastal States therefore react in the best self-interest when faced with the dilemma authorizing any entry into their ports, under a bilateral treaty obligation, which may be detrimental to them. This reaction tallies with the rights granted to coastal States in their territorial waters, and it can be onerous to challenge their claim that security and other interests were not threatened by the vessel which was denied entry.

However, a logical exception to this rule extends a right of passage and entry into port to vessels in distress. This right was established as far back as 1853 in international case law.[164] This right to seek refuge in a port may be justified by two main perspectives namely humanitarian considerations and *force majeure*. In the sea-migrants' protection quest however, it is only sensible to note that the humanitarian considerations constitute the principal basis of any right to seek refuge. Customary international law supports this posit through the ruling of Irish High Court of Admiralty stating that:

> In summary, therefore, I am satisfied that the right of a foreign vessel in serious distress to the benefit of a safe haven in the waters of an adjacent coastal state is primarily humanitarian rather than economic. It is not an absolute right. If safety of life is not a factor, then there is a widely recognized practice amongst maritime states to have regard to their own interests and those of their citizens in deciding whether or not to accede to any such request to enter.[165]

The humanitarian rationale maintains its relevance in the present context despite the fact that this ruling was passed in relation to a physically distressed

161 515 UNTS 205.

162 Article 2 of the Convention and Statute on the International Regime of Maritime Ports, 119 BFSP (1924) 568; 58 LNTS 287.

163 Aldo Chircop observes that though many States enter Bilateral agreements to guarantee port access, these agreements are not of a 'norm creating character' and do not establish a customary right of entry, *see* Aldo Chircop, 'Ships in Distress, Environmental Threats to Coastal States and Places of Refuge: New Directions for an Ancient Regime' (2002) 33 *Ocean Development and International Law* 210.

164 The Creole (1853), Moore, International Arbitration 824; and The Kate E. Hoff case (The Rebecca), (1929) VI RIAA 444.

165 The MV Toledo (1995) 2 ILRM 30, 48–9.

vessel which posed an environmental threat. Lord Stowell further buttresses this perception in *The Eleanor* by holding that 'the distress must be urgent, it must be something of grave necessity ... proved by the claimant in a clear and satisfactory manner ... there need not be immediate physical necessity, "moral necessity would justify the act".'[166] The above position provides a broader definition of distress which definitely augments the chances of vessels to gain access to ports.[167]

Besides the duty to render assistance to vessels and persons in distress, the flag State must take such measures necessary to ensure the vessel's safety at sea.[168] Article 94 (5) UNCLOS requires flag States to conform to generally accepted international regulations, procedures and practices, and to take any steps which may be necessary to secure their observation. However, SOLAS contemplates that the consequences of a rescue operation might be to render a vessel sea unworthy. It therefore provides that:

> Persons who are on board a ship by reason of force majeure or in consequence of the obligation laid upon the master to carry shipwrecked or other persons shall not be taken into account for the purpose of ascertaining the application to a ship of any provisions of the present convention.[169]

As such, SOLAS cannot be claimed as the basis of any right to enter the ports or disembark persons rescued at sea. This position is firmly reiterated by Article V-(b) SOLAS which preserves the right of a contracting party to control vessels which come into their ports, even in an emergency. In fact, a vessel can only logically claim a right of refuge only where unseaworthiness gives rise to a threat to human life.

Given the absence of any authoritative statement on the conditions for the exercise of the right, the discussion of the International Law Commission in respect of State responsibility, and in the decision of the tribunal in the Rainbow Warrior arbitration, enlightens the notion of distress stating that it:

166 1809, Edw 135.

167 An illustrative situation is that of the TAMPA which was a vessel in distress and so entitled to refuge. The Norwegian government and the owner of the Tampa declared it to be in violation of SOLAS because it did not have adequate safety equipment to deal with the asylum seekers. It was claimed that by picking up asylum seekers, the Tampa became subject to additional provisions of chapter III which rendered it sea unworthy. See UN Press Releases GA/9980 27 Nov 2001 and GA/9981 28 Nov 2001.

168 Article 94 (3) UNCLOS.

169 Article IV (b) SOLAS.

> [M]ay at most include a situation of serious danger, but not one that jeopardizes the very existence of the person concerned. The protection of something other than life, particularly where the physical integrity of the person is still involved, may admittedly represent an interest that is capable of severely restricting an individual's freedom of decision and induce him to act in a manner that is justifiable, although not in conformity with an international obligation of the State.[170]

Although the position of the ILC supports a wider definition of distress, it is not a guarantee that certain rights or immunities will be automatically applied.[171]

It should be noted that the right of entry into ports in distress was established in circumstances where such a course of action was the only one that might avoid an inevitable loss of life. In cases where multifarious options are available to the persons in distress, it becomes illogical to demand entry into a port since they may be required to take other available actions.[172] This approach remains consistent with the *sui generis* nature of the right of entry and respects any coastal State's decision to deny entry if it judges that the distress does not necessitate admission into its internal waters.[173]

Despite the laudable intention of international law which sets out obligations to protect those in distress, precision still cries for existence in numerous aspects since they are seldom implemented by States fully and consistently. Furthermore, coastal States enjoy great powers to regulate vessels and their activities in coastal waters. In the exercise of these powers, practical, commercial and security considerations often take primacy over humanitarian considerations. This constitutes a glaring reflection of the state of affairs of maritime law which needs to be ameliorated.

170 ILC, *ibid.*, 135, para. 10.

171 Some schools of thought distinguish true distress from self-inflicted distress. The element of volition characterizes self-inflicted distress and results in a loss of immunity from the coastal State jurisdiction, *see* DJ Devine, 'Ships in Distress – a judicial contribution from the South Atlantic' (1996) 20 *Marine Policy* 229.

172 The ILC refers to the element of choice, or rather the lack of choice as being a highly relevant consideration concerning distress, *see* ILC, n62, 133, para. 2.

173 It can equally be argued that if the reason for seeking entry into a port is to disembark asylum seekers in accordance with their demands, then the situation can be more appropriately termed duress rather than distress therefore justifying the decision of the coastal State to refuse entry.

Part 2: The Safe-Guarding of the Obligation of Assistance Even with the Smuggling of Migrants at Sea

The obligation of assistance as seen from the preceding analysis constitutes a pivotal aspect in the protection of migrants at sea. The ambit of this obligation comfortably spans civil and commercial activities carried out at sea, without excluding the socio-political push and pull factors that may force people to endanger themselves as migrants at sea thus necessitating the application of the obligation of assistance. It almost seems logical to erroneously exclude the criminal side of migration that systematically minimizes the human integrity of migrants yet goes unaddressed. Given the international nature of migration by sea, encountering a labyrinth of judicial, legal and political systems that address crimes such as human trafficking and smuggling varyingly is common. It therefore becomes almost easy to pardon anyone who intentionally overlooks the criminal activities that endanger migrants at sea with or without the consent of the migrant.

Despite the inherent complexities that motivate such a hasty pardon, the negative effects have however been attenuated by the Palermo Convention, the United Nations Convention against Transnational Organized Crime (UNTOC), which gives hope to migrants at sea even when ensnared by the intricacies of international crime. UNTOC is examined below in the light of the protection of migrants at sea.

2.1 *Overview of UNTOC*

UNTOC[174] is the main international instrument in the fight against transnational organized crime. UNTOC is appended by the Protocol to Prevent, Suppress and Punish Trafficking in Persons, Especially Women and Children;[175] the Protocol against the Smuggling of Migrants by Land, Sea and Air;[176] and the Protocol against the Illicit Manufacturing of and Trafficking in Firearms, Their Parts and Components and Ammunition.[177] UNTOC is arguably the pioneer

174 General Assembly Resolution 55/25 of 15 November 2000, entered into force on the 29th of September 2003, 2225 UNTS 209.

175 Protocol to Prevent, Suppress and Punish Trafficking in Persons, Especially Women and Children, adopted on the 15th of November 2000, entered into force 25 December 2003, 2237 UNTS 319.

176 Protocol against the Smuggling of Migrants by Land, Sea and Air, adopted on the 15 November 2000, entered into force 28 January 2004, 2241 UNTS 507.

177 Protocol Against the Illicit Manufacturing of and Trafficking in Firearms, Their Parts and Components and Ammunition, adopted on the 31 May 2001, entered into force 3 July 2005, 2326 UNTS 208.

global endeavour to encompass all concepts and measures required for the fight against organized crime in a single document. Despite almost close to twenty-five years of efforts by the UN to promote international cooperation in the combat against organized crime, it is only in recent years that a number of international meetings were oriented towards this direction.

The pivotal event in this light was the World Ministerial Conference on Organized Crime[178] whose political declaration and plan of action served as a basis for successive governmental meetings in Buenos Aires in 1995, Dakar in 1997 and Manila in 1998. These meetings focused on the need for an international convention, and acted as a forum for negotiations. The thorniest issues of debate included the definition of organized crime and the fear of developed States that the convention would be of little use as it would reflect the lowest common denominator. Based on the successive resolutions of the UN General Assembly, the text of UNTOC was negotiated by an *ad hoc* committee at ten sessions between 19 January 1999 and 28 July 2000 in the presence of both the non-governmental and intergovernmental organisations involved. On the 15th of November 2000, the General Assembly through resolution 55/25 adopted the text of UNTOC alongside the two Protocols on trafficking in human beings and smuggling of migrants which were later supplemented by the Protocol on trafficking in firearms. The UNTOC signing conference was finally held in Palermo between 12 and 15 December 2000, with 123 States signing and a large majority becoming Parties to its two protocols. The European Community signed as the first international organization. Under Article 36 UNTOC, 'regional economic integration organisations' are entitled to become parties to it, within the limits of their field of competence.

The effectiveness of UNTOC no doubt depends on its implementation, the making of the necessary changes to domestic legal systems and also by ensuring that law enforcement officers are aware of, and are properly trained to enforce the most innovative provisions.

2.2 *The Contents of UNTOC*

UNTOC is easily partitioned into four areas, namely criminalization, international cooperation, technical cooperation and implementation. Given the prickly issue of grasping the slippery concept of transnational organized crime in a definition that considers the legal and political perspectives, a twin approach was adopted. The negotiators judged it more appropriate to define the actors rather than their activities given the dynamic nature of transnational

178 Held in Naples, 21–23 November 1994.

organized activities depending on cost-benefit analysis. Thus, an organized criminal group was agreed to be:

> [A] structured group of three or more persons existing for a period of time and acting in concert with the aim of committing one or more serious crimes or offences established pursuant to the convention, in order to obtain, directly or indirectly, a financial or other material benefit.[179]

Secondly, based on the above definition, UNTOC strives to standardize offences as codified in national laws as a prerequisite of international cooperation. An *ad hoc* committee therefore ruminated on the appropriateness of the term 'serious crime' and the necessity of including a list of offences. Serious crime was eventually defined as 'conduct constituting a criminal offence punishable by a maximum deprivation of liberty of at least four years or a more serious penalty.'[180]

UNTOC procedes to establish four offences, namely participation in an organized criminal group, money laundering, corruption and obstruction of justice. Besides the offence of corruption that was considered a method and covered a very broad terrain thus necessitating a convention of its own,[181] the other offences are relatively wider in scope than national legislations cover.

UNTOC also defines transnationality. An offence is considered transnational in nature if it is committed in more than one state; if it is committed in one state but a substantial part of its preparation, planning, direction or control takes place in another State; or if it is committed in one state but involves an organized criminal group that engages in criminal activities in more than one state but has substantial effects in another State.

2.3 *UNTOC's Scope of Application*

An important addition to UNTOC concerns the provisions on extradition and mutual legal assistance that contain specific and very carefully-crafted language in order to facilitate the application of these articles and to establish both the transnationality and the involvement of an organized criminal group. The agreed solutions were based on the demonstrated political will of all countries involved in the process to conclude a convention that meets all their concerns. These solutions were also based on the shared desire to reach agreement without hurting the functionality and quality of the new instrument. To

179 Annex 1, Article 2(a) UNTOC.
180 Annex 1, Article 2(b) UNTOC.
181 General Assembly Resolution 55/61.

this effect, the provisions of UNTOC apply to the protocols unless otherwise specified or where the protocols contain provisions that specifically vary or are inconsistent with those of UNTOC. All protocol offences are equally considered as convention offences, which makes all convention provisions as to legal assistance applicable to cases that involve only protocol offences. The conference of States Parties, established by Article 32 UNTOC are to have similar functions for each protocol by the application of Article 32 to the Protocol in question, *mutatis mutandis*.

Articles 2 and 4 UNTOC set out the basic purpose and scope of the protocols. The protocols are intended to 'prevent and combat' trafficking in persons and facilitate international cooperation against such trafficking. It applies to the 'prevention, investigation and prosecution' of protocol offences, but only where these are 'transnational in nature' and involve an 'organized criminal group', as those terms are defined by UNTOC.

Despite the undeniable importance of the supporting protocols in the fight against transnational organized crime, only one of these protocols is relevant in the treatment of the topic which is the focus of this volume. The Protocol against trafficking in persons, especially in women and children, initially appears to warrant a more detailed treatment here, but the context and theme of this work pleads more for addressing a different protocol. The Protocol against Smuggling of Migrants by Land, Sea and Air (Smuggling Protocol) is unarguably on point with the demands of the protection of migrants at sea and deserves greater attention.

2.4 *The Preservation of the Obligation of Assistance in the Smuggling Protocol*

Given the vastness and magnitude of smuggling,[182] the Smuggling Protocol is examined here in its three main axes, namely general provisions, cooperation and preventive measures and finally the protection and assistance measures.

2.4.1 General Provisions of the Smuggling Protocol

These general provisions cover the definitions, criminalization, scope and purpose of the Smuggling Protocol that can be seen in its first six articles. Article 1 of the Smuggling Protocol lays down the relationship between transnational organised crime and the Protocol, complementing Article 37 UNTOC just as with the other protocols. These provisions should be interpreted

182 Protocol Against Smuggling of Migrants by land, Sea and Air, Supplementing the United Nations Convention Against Transnational Organized Crime, addresses smuggling through the three modes of transport.

simultaneously since the Smuggling protocol supplements UNTOC. Thus, the provisions of UNTOC apply to the Protocol directly unless otherwise specified or the Protocol contains provisions that specifically vary or are inconsistent with those of UNTOC. As a result, all offences envisaged by UNTOC are equally recognised by the Protocol. The Conference of States Parties established by Article 32 UNTOC therefore exercises similar functions for each protocol by the application of Article 32 of the Protocol in question. As laid down in the Smuggling Protocol, the 'purpose of this protocol is to prevent and combat the smuggling of migrants, as well as to promote cooperation among States Parties to that end, while protecting the rights of smuggled migrants.'[183]

Also of fundamental importance is the ensuing article that glaringly defines easily mistaken concepts and further clarifies the phenomenon of smuggling which greatly touches migrants at sea and hurts their integrity:

> For the purposes of this Protocol:
> a) 'Smuggling of migrants' shall mean the procurement, in order to obtain, directly or indirectly, a financial or other material benefit, of the illegal entry of a person into a State Party of which the person is not a national or a permanent resident;
> b) 'Illegal entry' shall mean crossing borders without complying with the necessary requirements for legal entry into the receiving State;
> c) 'Fraudulent travel or identity document' shall mean any travel or identity document:
> i. That has been falsely made or altered in some material way by anyone other than a person or agency lawfully authorized to make or issue the travel or identity document on behalf of a State; or
> ii. That has been improperly issued or obtained through misrepresentation, corruption or duress or in any other unlawful manner; or
> iii. That is being used by a person other than the rightful holder;
> d. 'Vessel' shall mean any type of water craft, including non-displacement craft and seaplanes, used or capable of being used as a means of transportation on water, except a warship, naval auxiliary or other vessel owned or operated by a Government and used, for the time being, only on government non-commercial service.[184]

183 Article 2 of the Smuggling Protocol.
184 Article 3 of the Smuggling Protocol.

From the above, the Smuggling Protocol applies only to the prevention, investigation or prosecution of such offences and the protection of the rights of persons who have been the objects of such offences. Worthy to note that the phrase 'persons who have been the object of such offences' in the Protocol provisions is intended to clarify the issue that smuggled migrants may be exploited or endangered by smugglers but do not necessarily constitute the 'victims' of the offence in the Protocol.

Article 6 of the Smuggling Protocol sets out a criminalization provision that requires States Parties to criminalise the smuggling of migrants as defined in Article 3, and enabling a person who is not a national or a permanent resident of a state to remain there illegally. Producing, procuring, providing, or possessing fraudulent travel or identity documents must also be made an offence, but exclusively in cases where these acts are committed for the purpose of smuggling migrants. Interestingly, this provision applies to smugglers excluding the illegal migrants who may only possess the documents for the purpose of use in their smuggling. The contents of Article 6 are laid out herein below for further clarity:

1. Each State Party shall adopt such legislative and other measures as may be necessary to establish as criminal offences, when committed intentionally and in order to obtain, directly or indirectly, a financial or other material benefit:
   a) The smuggling of migrants;
   b) When committed for the purpose of enabling the smuggling of migrants:
      i. Producing a fraudulent travel or identity document;
      ii. Procuring, providing or possessing such a document;
   c) Enabling a person who is not a national or a permanent resident to remain in the State concerned without complying with the necessary requirements for legally remaining in the State by the means mentioned in subparagraph
   d) of this paragraph or any other illegal means.
2. Each State Party shall also adopt such legislative and other measures as may be necessary to establish as criminal offences:
   a) Subject to the basic concepts of its legal system, attempting to commit an offence established in accordance with paragraph 1 of this article;
   b) Participating as an accomplice in an offence established in accordance with paragraph 1 (a), (b) (i) or (c) of this article and, subject to the basic concepts of its legal system, participating as an accomplice

in an offence established in accordance with paragraph 1 (b) (ii) of this article;
c) Organizing or directing other persons to commit an offence established in accordance with paragraph 1 of this article.

3. Each State Party shall adopt such legislative and other measures as may be necessary to establish as aggravating circumstances to the offences established in accordance with paragraph 1(a), (b)(i) and (c) of this article and, subject to the basic concepts of its legal system, to the offences established in accordance with paragraph 2(b) and (c) of this article, circumstances:
a) That endanger, or are likely to endanger, the lives or safety of the migrants concerned; or
b) That entail inhuman or degrading treatment, including for exploitation, of such migrants.

4. Nothing in this Protocol shall prevent a State Party from taking measures against a person whose conduct constitutes an offence under its domestic law.

The above situation subtly questions the position of the Smuggling Protocol to criminalising the smuggling of migrants without criminalizing the mere migration or the migrants themselves thus granting them an unfair protection. This situation is delicate because illegal migrants also commit offences related to illegal entry or residence in most countries, and are usually complicit in their own smuggling that is technically not addressed by the Smuggling Protocol. Articles 5 and 6(4) of the Protocol provide a relief from this dilemma by stating that the provisions of the Protocol and its implementing legislation should criminalise smuggling but not create any liability for having been smuggled,[185] but equally provides that offences or other measures adopted or applied by States Parties on their own authority could still apply to mere migrants. Lastly, Article 6(1) (b) makes clear that the provision is applicable exclusively to those who commit them for the purpose of smuggling others and not for their own migration.

In acknowledging the dangerous nature of smuggling and in an effort to increase the protection for migrants, States Parties are also required to legislate on smuggling circumstances that endanger the lives of migrants or their safety, or which entail inhuman or degrading treatment constitutes an aggravating circumstance.[186] This provision goes a long way to protect migrants at sea regardless of their status or legal situation.

185 Article 5 of the Smuggling Protocol.
186 Article 6(3) of the Smuggling Protocol.

Although the Smuggling Protocol applies to all forms of smuggling by land, air and sea, the volume of the problem and the body of international maritime law in existence imposes a special focus on smuggling by sea that further buttresses the theme of this work. Most of the provisions in this section addressing smuggling by sea seem inspired by earlier legislation on the boarding and searching of vessels and their related safeguards.[187]

This second part strives to empower States, faced with suspected migrant smuggling ships, to take actions to apprehend the migrants and smugglers and to preserve evidence, while respecting the sovereignty of the flag State.[188] This provision is justified by the fact that in many cases, vessels used to smuggle migrants are dilapidated or so sea unworthy that rapid action will be pivotal to preserving the safety of any migrants on board.

Under normal conditions, any action against a ship at sea can only be taken with the approval of the flag State of the ship. The Smuggling Protocol requires State parties to cooperate 'to the fullest extent possible' in accordance with the 'international law of the Sea', including the 1988 UN Convention on the LOS and other instruments.[189] The taking of measures against ships at sea is governed by Article 8 of the Smuggling Protocol, which envisages three basic cases.[190] The other provisions of Article 8 encourage cooperation and even envisage a situation where a State may solicit other States to take action against a suspected smuggling ship carrying its flag or registration number. Boarding and inspection authorisations may be granted but limits or conditions may be placed on what may be done (Article 8(4) and (5)). Such conditions must be respected unless lives are greatly endangered or there exists an agreement between the States involved stating otherwise.[191] In the absence of a nationality or registry, the ship may be boarded and inspected as necessary.

Article 9 of the Smuggling Protocol contains 'safeguard clauses' that limit the powers of State Parties to act under Article 8. The article also ensures that fundamental interests, such as the safe and humane treatment of persons found

---

187 Article 110 UNCLOS, Article 17 of the 1988 UN Convention against Illicit Traffic in Narcotic Drugs and Psychotropic Substances, as well as the 1988 Circular from the International maritime Organization titled Interim Measures for Combatting unsafe practices associated with the trafficking or transport of migrants by sea.

188 Article 8(2) of the Smuggling Protocol.

189 Article 7 of the Smuggling Protocol.

190 Article 8 of the Smuggling Protocol:
1. States seeking assistance against ships they believe to be their own (Art. 8 (1)),
2. States seeking permission to act against ships believed to be flagged or registered to another State (Art. 8(2)); and
3. States taking action against ships believed to be without nationality (Art. 8(7)).

191 Article 8(5) of the Smuggling Protocol.

on board vessels and the security of vessels and other cargoes, are protected. It preserves the existing jurisdictions of coastal States and the flag states of vessels, and provides compensation where the grounds for taking measures are later proven to be unfounded. Furthermore, any equipment used to take action must be clearly marked to identify it as being on government service when the action is taken.[192]

2.4.2 Cooperation and Prevention Measures

Prevention, co-operation and other measures are enshrined in Articles 10 to 18 of the Smuggling Protocol. In a similar manner as with the provisions of UNTOC,[193] the Protocol provides for the exchange of information that may range from general research or legislative information which would assist others in implementing the Protocol or combating smuggling more generally, as well as more specifically when sensitive information about specific smuggling cases are made available on techniques being used by smugglers.[194] As in the Protocol against Trafficking in Persons, specific legal and administrative measures to combat smuggling that involve commercial carriers are also required, 'to the extent possible'[195] in the Smuggling Protocol. These include penalties where carriers found carrying smuggled migrants are complicit or negligent as well as ensure that the requirements of carriers to check basic travel documents before transporting persons across international borders.

The use of false or fraudulent passports and other travel documents is an important element of smuggling, and documents are often taken from migrants upon arrival so that they can be re-used by the smugglers over and over again. Article 12 of the Smuggling Protocol that deals with the control and security of documents requires the use of travel documents that cannot be easily used by a person other than the legitimate holder, and of such quality that they cannot easily be falsified, altered or replicated. States Parties are further required to verify the legitimacy and validity of any documents purported to have been issued by them.[196]

Given the need to harmonise the applicable laws in both protocols on smuggling and trafficking, the requirements of Articles 12 and 13 are identical in both instruments. States Parties are called upon to undertake training

192 Article 9(4) of the Smuggling Protocol.

193 Articles 27, 28 and 29 UNTOC pertaining to the status of witnesses, cost of requests and treatment of evidence.

194 Article 10 of the Smuggling Protocol.

195 Article 11 of the Smuggling Protocol.

196 Article 13 of the Smuggling Protocol.

activities and adopt general preventive measures.[197] Training under Article 14 for officials can be domestic or in cooperation with other States Parties where appropriate. It must include not only methods and techniques for investigating and prosecuting offences, but also background intelligence-gathering, crime-prevention, and the need to provide humane treatment and respect for the basic human rights of migrants. Adequate resources are called for, with the assistance of other States where domestic resources or expertise are not enough as emphasized in Article 14(3).

Based on the assumption that a key element of prevention is the dissemination of information about the true conditions during smuggling and after arrival to discourage potential migrants, Article 15 of the Smuggling Protocol requires the creation or empowering of activities to gather such information, transmit it from one country to another, and ensure that it is made available to the general public and potential migrants. This completes Article 37 UNTOC which advocates for the dissemination of information intended for particularly vulnerable groups that are exposed to the activities of transnational organized crime like regional or ethnic groups likely to be solicited or recruited as potential migrants.

2.4.3 Protection and Assistance Measures under the Smuggling Protocol

The second part of the Smuggling Protocol equally examines the protection, assistance and return of migrants. Similar to the Protocol against Trafficking in Persons, these provisions take account of the fact that migrants, while often treated as a commodity by smugglers, are human beings whose rights must be respected and who must be protected from various forms of harm. Articles 16 (protection and assistance) and 18 (return) of the Smuggling Protocol provide for a basic assistance to smuggled migrants, taking into account the fact that they are not generally victims of crime and are in far less jeopardy of retaliation from traffickers, but also considering the fact that smuggling is often conducted in circumstances that endanger their lives or safety. As laid down more precisely by the Protocol:

1) In implementing this Protocol, each State Party shall take, consistent with its obligations under international law, all appropriate measures, including legislation if necessary, to preserve and protect the rights of persons who have been the object of conduct set forth in article 6 of this Protocol as accorded under applicable international law, in particular the right to life and the right not to be subjected to torture or other cruel, inhuman or degrading treatment or punishment.

197 Article 14 of the Smuggling Protocol.

2) Each State Party shall take appropriate measures to afford migrants appropriate protection against violence that may be inflicted upon them, whether by individuals or groups, by reason of being the object of conduct set forth in article 6 of this Protocol.
3) Each State Party shall afford appropriate assistance to migrants whose lives or safety are endangered by reason of being the object of conduct set forth in article 6 of this Protocol.
4) In applying the provisions of this article, States Parties shall take into account the special needs of women and children.
5) In the case of the detention of a person who has been the object of conduct set forth in article 6 of this Protocol, each State Party shall comply with its obligations under the Vienna Convention on Consular Relations, where applicable, including that of informing the person concerned without delay about the provisions concerning notification to and communication with consular officers.[198]

Several provisions of the Smuggling Protocol are intended to ensure that the basic human rights of migrants are protected from infringement, whether by traffickers, government officials or yet to be identified entities. The primary provision is Article 16, which requires appropriate legislative or other measures to 'preserve and protect' the rights of smuggled migrants. Article 14(2)(e) also requires the training of officials in 'the humane treatment of migrants and the protection of their rights', while Article 19 ensures that the rights of migrants and/refugees under other international humanitarian and human rights law are not affected by the Protocol. Article 16(5) even demands conformity with the provision of the Vienna Convention on Consular Relations[199] which requires States Parties to that instrument to inform apprehended migrants of their rights to consular access.

Other provisions in the Smuggling Protocol address concerns about dangerous conditions, degrading conditions or physical violence in the course of smuggling to which migrants are in many cases subjected. Article 16(2) of the Smuggling Protocol requires the adoption of appropriate measures to afford migrants protection against violence. Article 16(3) requires States Parties to create circumstances that endanger lives or safety or entail inhuman or degrading treatment in the course of smuggling, an aggravating circumstance to the basic smuggling offence, and Article 16(3) requires appropriate assistance to migrants whose lives or safety are endangered in the course of being

198 Article 16 entitled Protection and Assistance Measures of the Protocol against the Smuggling of Migrants by Land, Sea and Air.

199 Article 36 Vienna Convention on Consular Relations.

smuggled. The return of smuggled migrants to their countries of origin is dealt with in Article 18 of the Smuggling Protocol, which is similar but not identical to the corresponding provision (Article 6) of the Protocol against Trafficking in Persons.

Since migrants are less likely to be witnesses in transnational organized crime proceedings, the Protocol makes no specific provision for protection or participation in such proceedings, although migrants who are in this position would still be covered by Articles 24 and/or 25 UNCLOS, depending on the exact circumstances of their cases. The main protection envisaged for returning migrants requires all of the States Parties involved in the return operation of a migrant to ensure that it is carried out 'in an orderly manner and with due regard for the safety and dignity of the migrant.[200]

The provisions governing the repatriation or return of smuggled migrants and trafficking victims in both Protocols[201] are equally needed to specify the legal preconditions on which the right of destination States to return individuals and the obligations of countries of origin to facilitate and accept the return should be based. Despite unanimity that States Parties should be required to accept the return of their own nationals and permanent residents, views differed on whether the status of a smuggled migrant or trafficking victim should be determined at the time of entry into the State seeking to return the person or at the time of the actual return itself. The former option precludes States from revoking status as a national or resident to prevent the return, whereas the latter does not.

In the case of victims of trafficking, countries are obliged to accept the return of any person who is a national at the time of the return or who had a right of permanent residence at the time he or she entered the Destination State.[202] In the case of smuggled migrants, the obligation is only to accept those who are nationals or have a right of permanent residence at the time of the return,[203] although States Parties are also required to consider the return of migrants who had permanent residency rights at the time of entry into the State of their destination. The ground work for the Smuggling Protocol requires that States Parties 'would not deprive persons of their nationality contrary to international law, thereby rendering them stateless.' This acknowledges that nationality can be taken away for cause, but should not be taken away exclusively to prevent repatriation.

200 Article 18(5) of the Smuggling Protocol.
201 Article 18(1) (8) of the Smuggling Protocol.
202 Article 8(1) of the Smuggling Protocol.
203 Article 18(1) of the Smuggling Protocol.

Apart from these differences, the obligations placed on States concerning return or repatriation are the same in this instrument as in the Protocol against Trafficking in Persons. The basic obligation on States Parties is to 'facilitate and accept' the return of nationals or specified residents without undue delay and to verify without delay whether illegal migrants in other countries are in fact their nationals or residents.[204] This includes the obligation to issue any necessary travel documents such as passports, entry or transit visas. A combination of the above measures can comfortably be considered as synonyms to the duty to assist which has been carefully enshrined in UNTOC and the Protocols thereto.

SECTION 2: INTERNATIONAL LAW RECOGNIZES THE RIGHT TO SHELTER FOR ALL MIGRANTS BY SEA

The pressures and challenges posed by refugees arriving by sea have been age-old problems.[205] The most troubling issue about this problem is its unchanging nature. The crux of the matter remains the dilemma of reconciling the humanitarian plight of refugees and asylum seekers with the concerns of the destination States about illegal migration, mass migration of people, and the cost of asylum. The famous *Tampa* case[206] acutely highlighted the tension created between competing legal norms on one hand, and between moral and legal considerations on the other.

The facts in the *Tampa* case began on Sunday, 26 August 2001, when Captain Arne Rinnan of the MV Tampa, was asked by Australian Search and Rescue (AusSAR) to investigate a distress call from an Indonesian ferry in waters between Christmas Island and Indonesia. Responding to the request, Captain Rinnan found the vessel in immediate danger of sinking approximately 75 nm off Christmas Island. Although originally informed by AusSAR that the ferry had approximately 80 passengers, it turned out to be carrying 433 Afghan

---

204 Article 18(1) and (3) of the Smuggling Protocol.

205 Thousands of migrants fleeing Indo-China in the 1970s was documented by B. Grant, *The Boat People* (Melbourne Penguin 1980). Jewish refugees fleeing Nazi persecution was treated by G. Thomas and M. Morgan Witts, *The Voyage of the Damned* (London Coronet 1976). A more contemporary case is that of the United States of America which faced serious problems dealing with a large number of refugees from Cuba and Haiti, see B. Frelick, 'Haitian Boat Interdiction and Return; First Asylum and First Principles of Refugee Protection' (1993) 26 *Cornell International Law Journal* 675.

206 *See* E. Peyser, 'Pacific Solution'? The Sinking Right to Seek Asylum in Australia' (2002) 11 *Pacific Rim Law & Policy Journal* 431.

asylum seekers. After picking up the ferry passengers the Tampa resumed its voyage to Singapore. Captain Rinnan intended to make a detour to Indonesia to offload the passengers. However, considerable pressure from the passengers caused Captain Rinnan to send out two distress calls. He revealed that the health of the asylum seekers was deteriorating, several were unconscious and others were threatening to jump overboard if no medical assistance was provided. Under these circumstances Captain Rinnan decided to proceed to the asylum seeker's desired destination-Christmas Island. When Captain Rinnan gave notice of this intention to proceed to Christmas Island, permission to enter Australian waters was refused. This was ignored. In response, Australian troops were ordered to prevent the vessel from continuing. At 2 PM on 30 August these troops boarded and seized control of the Tampa. After a week-long standoff, during which time a lawsuit was issued against the Australian government, the rescuees were transferred to an Australian naval vessel and taken to Papua New Guinea where their asylum claims were processed. Subsequently, Australia reached an agreement, the so-called 'Pacific Solution' with New Zealand to take 150 asylum seekers and for Nauru to take the remainder, with the United Nations High Commission for Refugees processing the claims.

As seen in this case, it is therefore urgent to re-examine the available legal arsenal and project the rights available to migrants by sea and the considerations affecting the effective application of these rights. It can equally be purported that humanitarian considerations have not been granted due respect in the management of migrants at sea as will be argued below.

Part 3: The Right of Refuge for Any Shipwrecked Person

The pivotal rights that accurately embody and protect the right of refuge are unarguably the right of passage and the right of access to ports. It should be born in mind that these rights are sharply distinct from each other.[207] To this effect, ship masters transporting persons who have been rescued from distress at sea and who in turn lay claim to refugee status may wish to exercise these rights separately. More so, the application of certain human rights obligations on coastal States may have different implications on the different sections of the sea belonging to the coastal State as to whether they are internal waters, territorial seas or the contiguous zone.

207 Richard Barnes, 'Refugee Law at Sea' (2004) 53(1) *International and Comparative Law Quarterly* 47–77.

3.1 *Rights of Passage*

A coastal State enjoys unrivalled sovereignty over its territorial sea that spans a total distance of twelve nautical miles as enshrined by UNCLOS.[208] Logically, navigation constitutes the most used right exercised over the territorial sea. In order to humanize the use of this maritime area under the sovereignty of the coastal State, especially to the relief of distressed vessels, the right of innocent passage stipulates that a vessel may navigate the territorial sea without entering internal waters, and also includes the rights of entry and exit from port facilities and roadstead.[209] This provision insists that such passages must be 'continuous and expeditious' except for stopping and anchoring 'incidental to ordinary navigation or rendered necessary by force majeure or distress or for the purpose of rendering assistance to persons, ships or aircraft in danger or distress'. The pertinence of this provision in the present context in protecting rescued persons from shipwrecks and victims of other vessels in distress, is further buttressed by Article 24 UNCLOS:

> The coastal State shall not hamper the passage of innocent ships through the territorial sea except in accordance with this Convention. In particular, in the application of this Convention or of any laws or regulations adopted in conformity with this Convention, the coastal State shall not:
> a) Impose requirements on foreign ships which have the practical effect of denying or impairing the right of innocent passage; or
> b) Discriminate in any form or in fact against the ships of any State or against ships carrying cargoes to or from or on behalf of any State.[210]

It should however be noted that the above right can be suspended if it can be proven that the right of innocent passage had been suspended or even more importantly, that the passage was not innocent. To this effect, Article 19(1) UNCLOS provides that passage shall not be considered as innocent if it is prejudicial to the 'peace, good order or security of the coastal State'. Article 19(2) then proceeds to enlist certain activities that are considered as prejudicial. The appositeness of Article 19(2) (g) within the context of rescuing and offering refuge to victims in distress merits attention as it states that the passage of a vessel is rendered non-innocent if the vessel engages in 'the loading or unloading of any commodity, currency or person contrary to the customs, fiscal, immigration or sanitary laws and regulations of the coastal State'. For the

208 Articles 2 and 3 UNCLOS.
209 Article 18 UNCLOS.
210 Article 24(1) UNCLOS.

above to be enforced, the coastal State is required to give due publicity to any such laws and regulations affecting passage. The logic underlining this requirement is simply the importance of notifying foreign vessels of unknown local legislation that can potentially render passage non-innocent. It is worth noting that no such domestic laws exist in most cases so this approach to rendering innocent passage invalid is most often impossible.

However, the more probable scenario is to establish that rescued persons on board are unlawful immigrants. This alternative approach appears to be more enticing for coastal States with tough anti-immigration policies. Unfortunately for the followers of the illegal migrants approach, the argument hastily concludes on the status of the concerned migrants without any due legal process. This obviously contravenes the intentions of the 1951 Refugee Convention which provides that:

1. The Contracting States shall not expel a refugee lawfully in their territory save on grounds of national security or public order and pursuance of a decision reached in accordance with the process of law.
2. Each refugee shall be entitled, in accordance with the established law and procedure of the country, to submit evidence to clear himself and to be represented before the competent authority.
3. The Contracting State shall allow such refugee a reasonable period within which to seek legal admission into another country. The Contracting States reserve the right to apply during that period such internal measures as they deem necessary.[211]

Despite the above provision that quash the stereotypes and negative prejudgments that classify rescued migrants as illegal without due legal process, hardliners insist on drawing a difference between vessels commencing a voyage with the specific purpose of transporting illegal migrants and vessels stopping in the course of their journey to assist those in distress. While it is important to state that the former is entitled to due legal process while the latter deserves full assistance and cooperation from the concerned parties, it is even imperative to highlight that such distinctions are notably difficult and even fairly unworkable in practice. It therefore is inhumane to encourage distinctions of this nature that could eventually prove corrosive to asylum rights.

In addition to the open list of Article 19(2) UNCLOS enumerating the possible factors likely to be considered as security threats, the authority and appreciation of a potential security threat remains within the authority of the coastal State. In fact, it can only be hoped that this power of appreciation by the coastal State is exercised with the letter and spirit of the Convention as

211 Article 32 of the 1951 Refugee Convention.

only the coastal State can best appreciate the issues and circumstances that constitute a threat to its territory and proceed to legitimately suspend the right of passage. It should however be noted that despite the specific challenges that come with a large influx of asylum seekers, coastal States have, presently do and will continue to admit legions of asylum seekers into their territory. It will therefore be very improbable and even incongruous for a coastal State to claim that asylum-seeking in itself constitutes a menace to its peace and security. One legal scholar further argues that the difficulty with this argument lies in the fact that the conduct of a State in exercising its discretion cannot be presumed to give rise to an estoppel against a change in the exercise of that discretion. However, it may then be suggested that the State is not acting in accordance with the principle of good faith.[212]

Notwithstanding the above arguments, Article 25(3) UNCLOS still provides circumstances under which the right of innocent passage may still be temporarily suspended should the coastal State eventual decide that passage is not innocent:[213]

> The coastal State may, without discrimination in form or in fact among foreign ships, suspend temporarily in specified areas of its territorial sea the innocent passage of foreign ships as such suspension is essential for the protection of its security, including weapons exercises. Such suspension shall take effect only after having been duly published.

As stated in Article 25(3), the conditions for suspension include the requirement that they must be non-discriminatory and must be duly published. However, what constitutes due publicity is left undefined and abandoned to the discretion of the coastal State. Although coastal States enjoy a relatively wide margin of discretion in deciding what constitutes a threat, the measure taken in response will be subject to requirements of necessity and proportionality.[214] It can therefore be concluded that the exercise of sovereignty by the coastal State over its territorial sea is subject to certain restrictions drawn from both jurisprudence and legislation. Where these restrictions are absent or liable to ambiguous interpretations, the coastal State is presumed to have the full

212 Richard Barnes, 'Refugee law at Sea' (2004) 53(1) *International and Comparative Law Quarterly* 11.

213 Article 25(1) UNCLOS.

214 G.S. Goodwin-Gill, '*The Refugee in International law*' (2nd edition, Oxford University Press 1996) 162.

authority to act. These restrictions curb abuses and facilitate the granting of refuge to rescued persons in danger at sea through the right of passage.

3.2 *Access to Ports*

Given the fact that innocent passage does not imply a parallel right of entry into ports, it will be important to examine the right of access to ports as earlier stated. As reiterated by case law, ports constitute a part of internal waters and fall under the regime of sovereignty of the coastal State.[215] With the above in mind, the right of entry remains a privilege to be granted by the coastal State unless there exists a bilateral or multilateral treaty between concerned parties addressing any such entry.[216]

It is fairly embarrassing to observe that despite the pertinence of the right of access to ports, the quasi-totality of contemporary maritime legal instruments fail to address this issue. Neither the Convention on the Territorial Sea and the Contiguous Zone,[217] nor UNCLOS establish a right of entry into foreign ports. However, there is a provision for a reciprocal right of access to, and equality of treatment between ports enshrined in the 1923 Maritime Ports Convention.[218] Sadly enough, this Convention suffers from a negligent amount of ratification and can hardly be considered representative enough to influence customary international law.

Besides, in cases where ports are open or where the rights of entry are enshrined in a treaty, coastal States still retain the right to reject entry where it judges its vital interests to be under serious threats as clearly provided for in Article 16 of the Maritime Ports Convention. Some other legal instruments even raise the bar a little higher by denying entry into their ports on the basis of 'public morality, order, and security or to prevent the introduction or spread of disease or pests affecting public health, animals, or plants'.[219] It is equally not surprising that early academic doctrinal opinion predominantly defended

215 The International Court of Justice affirmed in the Nicaragua case that internal waters are subject to the sovereignty of the state and that it is 'by virtue of its sovereignty that the coastal State may regulate access to its ports', *see* ICJ Reports (1986) 14 at paras. 212–13.

216 Some scholars claim that despite the entry of States into Agreements to guarantee port access, their agreements do not establish a customary right of entry because the agreements are not of a 'norm creating character', *see* A. Chircop, 'Ships in Distress, Environmental Threats to Coastal States and places of Refuge: New Directions for an Ancient Regime' (2002) 33 *Ocean Development and International Law* 207, 210.

217 515 UNTS 205.

218 Article 2 of the Convention and Statute on the International Regime of Maritime ports, 119 BFSP (1924) 568; 58 LNTS 287.

219 Article 5(2) of the Convention for the Facilitation of Internal Maritime Traffic.

the thesis of States having the power to limit entry into their ports.[220] It was therefore only logical to consider the actions of States founded and adequate to justify the closure of their ports to foreigners.

There is however a glimpse of hope that can be used as the lone exception to this rule which greatly limits the protection of distressed migrants at sea in search of a place of refuge. This lone exception extends the right of passage and entry into ports to vessels in distress. Very early jurisprudence established this right as far back as 1853 and 1929 in the cases of the *Creole*[221] and the *Rebecca*[222] respectively. These cases derived two justifications in support of the right to seek refuge in a port, namely broad humanitarian considerations on one hand and force majeure or circumstances beyond the control of mariners on the other hand. The humanitarian considerations however take primacy as principal justification for the right to seek refuge as laid out by more recent case law:

> In summary, therefore, I am satisfied that the right of a foreign vessel in serious distress to the benefit of a safe haven in the waters of an adjacent coastal State is primarily humanitarian rather than economic. It is not an absolute right. If safety of life is not a factor, then there is a widely recognised practice among maritime states to have regard to their own interests and those of their citizens in deciding whether or not to accede to any such request to enter port.[223]

The humanitarian argument posited by Justice Barr in the above decision fits squarely with the context of this theme. Another legal opinion props the humanitarian approach by detailing that the 'distress must be urgent, it must be something of a grave necessity ... proved by the claimant in a clear and satisfactory manner ... there need not be immediate physical necessity ... moral necessity would justify the act'.[224] This remarkably broader perception of distress offers a greater chance of obtaining access to ports for vessels in distress.

Apart from the duty to render assistance to vessels and persons in distress, international legislation requires that flag States must take all necessary measures to ensure the vessel's safety at sea.[225] UNCLOS goes even further to

220 McDougal and W.T. Burke, *The Public Order of the Oceans* (New Haven Yale University Press 1962) 93.

221 *The Creole v. Great Britain* (1853) General Claims Commission, Umpire M. Bates deciding.

222 Kate A. Hoff, Administratix of the Estate of Samuel B. Allison, deceased (USA) v. United Mexican States, (April 2. 1929) General Claims Commission concerning the ship *Rebecca*, Commissioner Nielson deciding.

223 Barr J., Irish High Court of Admiralty, *The MV Toledo*, 1995, 2 ILRM 30, pp. 48–9.

224 Lord Stowell, *The Eleanor* (1809), Edw 135.

225 Article 92(1) UNCLOS.

require that the flag State should 'conform to generally accepted international regulations, procedures and practices, and to take any steps which may be necessary to secure their observation'.[226]

In situations where States claim to be fulfilling their international obligations by ensuring rescue and bringing the rescued to persons to the closest port that is usually away from the port of the rescuing State, SOLAS anticipates that such a rescue operation may render the vessel unseaworthy and further endanger the lives of the concerned in distress. It therefore provides accordingly:

> Persons who are on board a ship by reason of force majeure or in consequence of the obligation laid upon the master to carry shipwrecked or other persons shall not be taken into account for the purpose of ascertaining the application to a ship of any provisions of the present Convention.[227]

The above provision affirms the fact that SOLAS cannot be cited as a basis for claiming any right to enter the ports or disembark persons rescued at sea. However, it provides even better protection for the rescued persons by insisting that SOLAS will not apply to shipwrecked, coerced and other persons faced with conditions of force majeure. This is reaffirmed by Article V(b) SOLAS which preserves the right of a contracting party to control vessels that come into their ports, even in an emergency. This does not change the fact that unseaworthiness is different from distress and should not be used as a reason to deny distressed persons entry into a port. Only where unseaworthiness gives rise to a threat to human life may the vessel claim a right of refuge.

The deafening silence of any authoritative voice facilitating the exercise of this right is easy to observe. Conversely, the works of the International Law Commission on State Responsibility can be relied upon alongside case law[228] to further enlighten the notion of distress. The International Law Commission therefore perceives that a situation of distress:

226 Article 95(5) UNCLOS.

227 Article IV(b) SOLAS.

228 Rainbow Warrior (New Zealand v France), France new Zealand Arbitration tribunal of 30 April 1990. International Law Reports (1990) 499. Distress is discussed as a circumstance precluding international responsibility but remains applicable to the case. The decision of the Tribunal relies on the commentary of the International law Commission which equally got inspiration from maritime practice, *see* (1973) Yearbook of International Law Commission, vol. II, 134, para. 4.

> [M]ay at most include a situation of serious danger, but not one that necessarily jeopardizes the very existence of the person concerned. The protection of something other than life, particularly where the physical integrity of a person is still involved, may admittedly represent an interest that is capable of severely restricting an individual's freedom of decision and induce him to act in a manner that is justifiable, although not in conformity with an international obligation of the State.[229]

The above doctrinal position of the International Law Commission therefore considers distress to include 'the existence of very exceptional circumstances of extreme urgency involving medical or other considerations of an elementary nature', thereby giving a broader definition to distress without necessarily creating any rights or immunities.

The right of vessels in distress to seek refuge in ports was devised to justify circumstances in which such entry was the sole course of action available to avoid an inevitable loss of life. This argument becomes clearly unconvincing for situations of distress that may be avoided by other courses of action. It is even trendy for coastal States to activate this argument by drawing a distinction between true distress and self-inflicted distress. This distinction introduces the element of volition in self-inflicted distress thus cancelling the immunity from coastal State jurisdiction. But as earlier stated, such distinctions are void of the highly coveted humanitarianism in the sea that makes the distinction irrelevant once distress is established and most importantly, such distinctions suffer from practical inaccuracies rendering the distinction stereotype and full of prejudgments.[230] In other words, the availability of alternative actions to persons in distress may lead to a justified denial of entry by the coastal State.

It is an equally disputable argument to claim that if the reason for seeking entry into a port is to disembark asylum seekers in accordance with their demands, then a concrete case of duress can be established instead of distress and the coastal State will be in its full rights to deny entry into its port. Despite the efforts by international law and doctrine to protect persons in distress, a mammoth effort is still required to render certain aspects precise enough and facilitate application as for the time being, they are neither fully nor consistently applied. In addition, the vast rights enjoyed by coastal States tend to favour practical, commercial and security considerations at the expense of humanitarian considerations that are highly preached.

229 International Law Commission, *ibid.*, 135, para. 10.

230 D.J. Devine, 'Ships in Distress – A judicial contribution from the South Atlantic' (1996) 20 *Marine Policy* 229.

3.3 *Appraisal of the Right of Refuge*

The above discussion projects two main issues, namely the right to determine whether a vessel enjoys the right of innocent passage in the territorial waters of a State, and secondly, how to determine whether a vessel is in distress and consequently has the right to call at a port in order to disembark passengers. In either case, the law portrays gaping loopholes. The ambiguous definition of obligations leads to very timid implementation. The same can be said of the rights of refuge.

The intransigence of numerous coastal States creates untold problems for those in distress and those rendering assistance. This inevitably leads to a vital disrespect for the moral and legal obligations to provide assistance to those in distress at sea. The dysfunctional coexistence of the rights and duties is portrayed by the obligation to provide assistance to persons in need of rescue alongside the quasi-inexistence of an obligation to receive the rescued persons.

The overwhelming powers of coastal States to control activities in their coastal waters makes the situation even more challenging. The human rights perspective however offers an escape vent by creating circumstances under which States denying refuge to vessels in distress will be violating fundamental human rights obligations. Greater concern is therefore placed on the safety of persons in distress at sea. Refugee interests are granted primacy given their greater exposure to risks. In order to ensure the effectiveness of this protection, cooperation and burden-sharing that can be associated to more practical, unambiguous and authoritative legislation appears to be most feasible. Redefining the rights and duties of coastal States and other concerned parties will guarantee greater protection for persons in need of international protection. To achieve this, sovereign responsibilities and policy developments seem indispensable should the above and other rights stand a chance of proper application.

3.4 *The Provision of a 'Place of Safety' in Any State of Disembarkation*

Due to their geo-strategic locations, certain coastal States have become privileged entry points for numerous migrants and refugees who manage to cross the seas in search of their final destination. Existing data envisages a constant increase of these migrants at sea, with the often sea unworthy ships used for this migration, with a continuing need for rescue at sea for the States in which they land to offer assistance and asylum.[231] The obligation to offer assistance

231 UN Refugee Agency (UNHCR) <http://data.unhcr.org/mediterranean/regional,php> accessed 30 June 2023.

should ultimately ensure the safety of the rescued persons. The provision of such safety is usually referred to as the provision of a 'place of safety', whose conception, perception and application has given rise to dense ambiguity. Though often considered a right, it cannot be imputed on States as an obligation due to the complete absence or timid existence of authoritative legal voices to this effect. This right is examined herein below through another concept, embarkation, which was long ignored by the maritime international community.

3.4.1 The Embarkation Dilemma

The legal obligation to render assistance to persons in distress at sea is consecrated by both customary international law[232] as well as treaties.[233] It should be underlined that no State can use its sovereign powers to ignore the application of this obligation in its territorial sea.[234] To this effect, flag States are required to rapidly run to the assistance of ships in distress when informed while coastal States are called upon to establish, operate and maintain adequate and effective search and rescue services. It is however disheartening to note that neither treaty nor customary law requires States letting these rescued persons disembark onto their territory.

Both SOLAS and the International Convention on Maritime Search and Rescue provide that States must arrange for the disembarkation of persons rescued at sea as soon as reasonably practicable.[235] The State in charge of the search and rescue region (SRR) in which survivors are recovered is held responsible for providing a place of safety on its own territory or ensuring that such a place of safety is granted in another country.[236] The document[237] proceeds to define place of safety as:

232 UN Commission on International Law, 'Commentary on Draft Article 12 of the United Nations Convention on the High Seas' (1956) UN Doc. A/3179, see also Kyriaki Noussia, 'The Rescue of migrants and Refugees at Sea: Legal Rights and Obligations' (2017) 31 *Ocean Year Book* 155–170.

233 Articles 58(2) and 98(1) UNCLOS.

234 MSC 76/22/8. 'Any other business. Review of safety measures and procedures for the treatment of persons rescued at sea', 31 July 2002, Annex: 'Report-Record of Decisions on the United Nations Inter-Agency Meeting on the Treatment of persons Rescued at Sea', para. 6; and Richard Barnes, 'Refugee Law at Sea' (2004) 53(1) *International and Comparative Law Quarterly* 47–77 at 50–52.

235 Chapter v Regulation 33 SOLAS and Chapter 3 para. 3.1.9 SAR.

236 MSC Res. 167 (78) Annex 34: 'Guidelines on the Treatment of Persons Rescued at Sea' (20 May 2004) at para. 2.5.

237 *Ibid.*, note 30.

[A]s a location where rescue operations are considered to terminate;
- Where the survivor's safety or life is no longer threatened,
- Basic human needs (such as food, shelter and medical needs) can be met,
- Transportations arrangements can be made for the survivors' next or final destination.[238]

It should be noted from the above that States owe no duty to disembark rescued persons even if the assisting ship may only serve as a temporary place of safety. A State can therefore deny any disembarkation onto its own territory or make this dependent on certain conditions[239] thereby denying the rescued migrants' right to a place of safety.

This state of affairs has resulted in a very morbid practice wherein, persons rescued at sea can spend weeks or even months on a ship at sea before a State allows them to go ashore. The most logical reason for this reluctance is the fact that almost all the rescued persons are migrants requesting asylum. More so, the migration is of a mixed nature involving political migrants and refugees trying to reach a safe shore.[240] States are therefore reticent to permit disembarkation unless they receive financial or readmission guarantees. Unfortunately, negotiations on these issues can last for weeks or even months. This implies that migrants in need of medical care and other immediate needs do not receive the due aid immediately.[241] Given the limited means and inherent costs on the commercial ships such as delay, it is common practice for shipmaster to

238 Guidelines on the Treatment of Persons Rescued at Sea, para. 6.12.

239 G.S. Goodwin-Gill, *The Refugee in International Law* (Clarendon Press, Oxford 1996) 157.

240 Jasmine Coppens & Eduard Somers, 'Towards New Rules on Disembarkation of Persons Rescued at Sea?' (2010) 25(3) *The International Journal of Marine and Coastal Law* 377–403.

241 The case of the *Marine I* provides such an example. On 30 January 2007, the Spanish Coast Guard received a distress call from the vessel *Marine L.* It was alleged that over 300 migrants from Guinea were on board. Although the *Marine I* was within the Senegalese SRR, Senegal requested Spain to proceed with a rescue operation, claiming that Senegal did not have the proper means to assist. Because the Mauritanian port of Nouadhibou was closest to the emergency, Senegal also informed Mauritania of the situation. On 4 February, a Spanish maritime rescue tug reached the *Marine I* and provided immediate relief by handing out supplies of water and food. The Spanish government also commenced negotiations with Senegal and Mauritania on the fate of the migrants. On 12 February (two weeks after the distress call), Spain, Senegal and Mauritania finally reached an agreement regarding the passengers. It was reportedly agreed that Spain would pay €650,000 in return for Mauritania allowing the passengers to disembark. Repatriation commenced the day after the migrants had disembarked. Guinea agreed to readmit thirty-five passengers, all of African origin.' In total, Spain reported 18,000 irregular arrivals by sea from West Africa that year. The fact that Spain was prepared to pay as

ignore migrants at sea and even distress calls in total violation of international law because they know that their entrance into ports will be refused.

In 2009, the Facilitation Committee (FAL) of the International Maritime Organization (IMO) approved a circular on 'Principles relating to the administrative procedures for disembarking persons rescued at sea'.[242] The Circular aimed at amending SOLAS and SAR, taking into account these principles as appropriate. These principles deserve a closer look in the subsequent paragraphs on the legal context given their pertinence in the protection of migrant rights at sea with respect to providing a place of safety.

3.4.2 The Legal Framework of Disembarkation

It is worth mentioning that the legal framework of disembarkation has a historical background that should not be overlooked. This historical background can be traced as far back as the communist regime of Vietnam in the 1970s that engendered the phenomenon of the boat people. In collaboration with many States, the United Nations High Commission for Refugees (UNHCR) initiated the Disembarkation Resettlement Offers Scheme (DISERO) in 1979[243] which was closely followed by the Rescue at Sea Resettlement Offers Scheme (RASRO) in 1985.[244] With an ever-increasing number of refugees and a corresponding decline in the willingness of coastal States to offer protection and a safe place due to the pools of 'long-stayers', a Comprehensive Plan of Action (CPA) was drafted in 1989 by the Steering Committee of the International Conference on Indo-Chinese Refugees.[245] A primary objective of the CPA was to identify the Status of migrants and to resettle exclusively those with a refugee status in harmony with the 1951 Refugee Convention. This implied that those without refugee status were promptly repatriated and reintegrated into their home countries. Unlike with the DISERO programme, the CPA involved the countries of origin and was terminated in 1996 because its objectives were considered to have been met.

---

much as €650,000 to prevent the disembarkation of 300 migrants shows that some States are reluctant to allow disembarkation of rescued persons onto their territory.

242 FAL 3/Circ.194 'Principles Relating to Administrative Procedures for Disembarking Persons Rescued at Sea' (22 January 2009).

243 United Nations, International Conference on Indo-Chinese Refugees, 20–21 July 1979, Geneva; and UNGA, 'Report of the Secretary General on the Meeting on Refugees and Displaced Persons in South East Asia and Subsequent Developments', UN Doc, A/34/627.

244 UNHCR EXCOM, Sub-Committee on International Protection, 'Problems Related to the Rescue of Asylum Seekers in Distress at Sea' 1st September 1983, UN Doc. EC/SCP/30.

245 United Nations, International Conference on Indo-Chinese Refugees, 13–14 June 1989, Geneva; UNGA, 'Report of the Secretary General on Indo-Chinese refugees; and Annex: Declaration and Comprehensive Action Plan (CPA), UN Doc. A/44/523.

This painful precedent demonstrates the aching insufficiency of the international legal framework in resolving the disembarkation problem and by extension the issue of providing a place of safety.[246] This state of affairs inspired the creation of an Interagency Group to deal with the problems of migrants at sea.[247] This group comprised IMO, UNHCR, UNDOALOS,[248] United Nations office on Drugs and Crime (UNODC), United Nations Office of the High Commissioner for Human Rights (OHCHR) and the International Organization for Migration (IMO). It is worth noting that the competences of IMO and UNDOALOS extend to the search-and-rescue aspects as well as to the provision of a place of safety. UNDOALOS equally deals with cooperation and coordination of law of the sea issues within the framework of the UN General Assembly.[249] The competences of the other organizations are considered to be global and multi-disciplinary given their relation asylum, transnational organized crime such as human trafficking, human rights and migration.

The current legal framework can be said to have been inspired by satisfaction obtained from the preceding interagency gatherings. The legal arsenal was therefore enriched by documents such as SOLAS and SAR Amendments,[250] the IMO Guidelines on the Treatment of Persons Rescued at Sea[251] and the IMO/UNHCR practical guide on rescue at sea.[252]

The above legal documents target the protection of the rights and interests of concerned parties like rescued persons, flag States, coastal States, ship master etc. These ratified amendments aim at guiding stakeholders in the accomplishment of their duties. The practical guide acts as a manual for concerned parties especially during the post rescue phase. It contains obligatory procedures alongside applicable principles of international law including the law of the sea and others, and finally relevant counsel and contact information.

246 *See* Cecilia Baillet, 'The Tampa Case and Its Impact on Burden Sharing at Sea' (2003) 25(3) *Human Rights Quarterly* 759.

247 First Interagency Group Meeting 'The Treatment of Persons Rescued at Sea', Geneva, 2–3 July 2002; and MSC 76/22/8.

248 UNDOALOS is United Nations Division for Ocean Affairs and the Law of the Sea.

249 UNGA Res. 49/28 of 6th December 1994, UN Doc. A/RES/49/28, Annex para.26.

250 The 2004 Amendments to SOLAS (MSC Res. 153 (78): Adoption of Amendments to the International Convention for the Safety of Life at Sea, 1974, as Amended on the 20th of May 2004. SAR Conventions (MSC Res. 155(78): Adoption of Amendments to the International Convention on maritime Search and Rescue, 1979, amended in May 2004 and entered into force on the 1st of January 2006.

251 MSC Res. 167(78) Annex 34.

252 IMO/UNHCR, 'Rescue at sea. A guide to Principles and Practice as Applied to Migrants and Refugees', 2006.

The 2004 SOLAS Amendments equally allude to the situation of rescued persons in relation to the obligation of assistance that should apply, regardless of the nationality, status and circumstances in which the rescued persons are found.[253] Again, all embarked persons should be treated with humanity within the capabilities and limitations of the ship.[254] Furthermore, neither actors, stakes nor circumstances should impact the professional decision of the ship to the detriment of the safety of life at sea.[255] In addition, other remote causes linked to contractual obligations and cost should not be used to minimize the humanitarian duties of the ship or the coastal State in relation to embarkation rights in particular and the safety of migrants in general. Finally, SOLAS highlights the importance of arranging for disembarkation as soon as reasonably practicable.[256] In the same line, the IMO Guidelines on the Treatment of Persons at Sea lay down that the State Authorities responsible for the safe search and rescue in which survivors were recovered is responsible for the provision of a place of safety or ensuring that such a place of safety is duly provided.[257]

3.4.3 Appraisal of the Provision of a Place of Safety

Denying the solid impact created by the existing legal arsenal as to the provision of a place of safety would be insincere. However, it would also be counter-productive to deny the persistent existence of problematic issues that bedevil the protection of migrants at sea. For one thing, the implementation of the 2004 SOLAS and SAR Amendments has been relatively ineffective. Some States are still yet to sign the amendments while others find implementation too costly in every perspective be it social, economic or even political. This pushes most ship masters to ignore migrant vessels in distress or simply tow their boats into the rescue zone of another country as reported by the European Council on Refugees and Exiles (ECRE).[258] This behaviour questions the efficacy of these legal instruments like the IMO Guidelines that is mostly soft law with no veritable binding obligation.

253 Chapter V, Regulation 33, Para. 1 SOLAS.

254 Para. 6 SOLAS.

255 Ibid.

256 Para. 34-1 SOLAS.

257 MSC Res. 167 (78) Annex 34.

258 MSC 84/20/1 'Report-Record of Decisions on the Third United Nations Inter-Agency Meeting on the Treatment of Persons Rescued at Sea' (1 February 2008), Annex, para. 12, also European Council on Refugees and Exiles (ECRE) 'What Price Does a Refugee Pay to Reach Europe?' (10 February 2009) <https://documentation.lastradainternational.org/lsidocs/ECRE_Access_Case_Studies_Feb_09.pdf> accessed 30 June 2023.

SOLAS and SAR stipulate that disembarkation must be arranged as soon as reasonably practicable and that the State responsible for the rescue has the primary responsibility for providing a place of safety and ensuring that such a place of safety is provided. However, these provisions neither constitute nor imply an obligation for States to disembark rescued persons on their territory that they can make dependent on numerous internal conditions. The trendy approach is to share the costs of disembarking migrants among the concerned States through agreements. Unfortunately, not all countries have materialized such agreements so the duration of disembarkation can still be sadly lengthy to the detriment of rescued migrants.

Given the morbid duration between rescue and disembarkation, it is important to highlight the clear absence of the ambits of the responsibility of contracting parties who are not responsible for the safety-research-rescue operation in which the rescue occurs. Again, in areas with overlapping zones of responsibility, it is unclear which contracting State should be primarily responsible for finding a suitable place of safety.[259]

In 2007, the Interagency Group discussed the issue of disembarkation of migrants rescued at sea and the IMO announced that its FAL Committee was in the process of harmonizing the procedures on disembarkation so to render them more predictable and efficient. For two years, 2007–2009, the FAL Committee identified five principal aspects of an elective character that States could incorporate into their domestic administrative procedures for the disembarkation of persons rescued at sea as follows:

1. The coastal State should ensure that the search and rescue (SAR) service or other competent national authority coordinates its efforts with all other entities responsible for matters relating the disembarkation of persons rescued at sea;
2. It should also be ensured that any operations and procedures such as screening and status assessment of rescued persons that go beyond rendering assistance to persons in distress are to be carried out after disembarkation to a place of safety. The master should normally only be asked to aid such processes by obtaining information about the name, age, gender, apparent health and medical condition and any special medical needs of any person rescued. If a person rescued expresses a wish to apply for asylum, great consideration must be given to the security of the asylum seeker. When communicating this information, it should

259 FSI 17/15/2 'Measures to Protect the Safety of Persons Rescued at Sea. Comments on Document FSI 17/15/1. Submitted by Malta' (27 February 2009), paras. 9–12 available in the IMO database, docs.imo.org.

therefore not be shared with his or her country of origin or any other country in which he or she may face threat;

3. All parties involved (for example, the Government responsible for the SAR area where the persons are rescued, other coastal States in the planned route of the rescuing ship, the flag State, the ship-owners and their representatives, States of nationality or residence of the persons rescued, the State from which the persons rescued departed, if known, and the United Nations High Commissioner for Refugees (UNHCR)) should cooperate in order to ensure that disembarkation of the persons rescued is carried out swiftly, taking into account the master's preferred arrangements for disembarkation and the immediate basic needs of the rescued persons. The Government responsible for the SAR area where the persons were rescued should exercise primary responsibility for ensuring such cooperation occurs. If disembarkation from the rescuing ship cannot be arranged swiftly elsewhere, the Government responsible for the SAR area should accept the disembarkation of the persons rescued in accordance with immigration laws and regulations of each Member State into a place of safety under its control in which the persons rescued can have timely access to post rescue support;
4. All parties involved should cooperate with the Government of the area where the persons rescued have been disembarked to facilitate the return or repatriation of the persons rescued. Rescued asylum seekers should be referred to the responsible asylum authority for an examination of their asylum request; and
5. International protection principles as set out in international instruments should be followed.[260]

Despite the general support for these principles, some States like the United States of America emitted reserves to certain points that they judged too far-reaching and detrimental to their interests and fundamentally inconsistent with its domestic laws. The third Principle was unsparingly criticised. It stated that 'When disembarkation cannot be arranged swiftly elsewhere, the Government of the SRR should accept – in accordance with national immigration laws and regulations – to disembark the persons rescued'. The logical interpretation of this principle is that coastal States have total responsibility which was judged unacceptable by most coastal States. To this effect, some other countries raised their objections in relation to embarkation procedures

260 FAL 35/Circ. 194 'Principles Relating to Administrative Procedures for Disembarking Persons Rescued at Sea' (22 January 2009), para. 2 available in the IMO database, docs.imo.org.

and the stay of rescued migrants.[261] Besides the above, the other FAL principles already existed in non-binding legal instruments like the IMO Guidelines on the Treatment of Persons Rescued at Sea and the IMO/UNHCR Practical Guide on Rescue at Sea. It is worth noting that they can attain a binding status if they are used as basis for amendment of SOLAS or SAR.

The urgent necessity of providing a place of safety evidently reposed on the issue of disembarkation as was observed by stakeholders after several technical meetings on the issue. In fact, the participants of the fourth Interagency Group Meeting of 2008 opined that if States failed to meet their obligations, the masters of ships could not fulfil their duties either. Given the varying interests of the stakeholders, any ideal legislation should reflect the interests of the ship, flag States, coastal States and migrants. This is of course a herculean order.

It should first and foremost be observed that there is no express obligation for States to disembark migrants in international law. Therefore, accepting such an obligation will imply ceding a reasonable part of State sovereignty though susceptible to modifications by treaty agreements. This is justified by the fact that disembarkation takes place in coastal waters that are located in the internal waters on States thus subject to domestic law.[262]

Judicial precedent has attempted a conditional waiver of State sovereignty in relation to the issue of disembarkation but with relative success. The ruling in the 1958 *Aramco* case between Saudi Arabia and the Arabian American Oil Company (ARAMCO) held that '[a]ccording to a great principle of public international law the ports of every State must be open to foreign merchant vessels and can only be closed when the vital interests of the State so require'.[263] This ruling subtly forges a right to access for merchant vessels carrying persons rescued at sea even when these are migrants. However, this ruling errs by the mere fact that there is no proof of such a principle in international law.[264] Despite the occasional entry permission granted to merchant vessels by most States for economic reasons, such bilateral agreements cannot be attributed a legislative status at international level. With the existence of a legal vacuum, states can logically legislate on the conditions for access into their ports. Some early treaties hinge on the non-discrimination principle to regulate access to

---

261 This was notably the case with Malta and Japan. *See* FAL 35/*WP.5* 'Formalities connected with the Arrival, Stay and Departure of Persons' (14 January 2009), para. 6 available in the IMO database, docs.imo.org.

262 Nicaragua case (Nicaragua v. USA) [1986] ICJ Rep., paras. 212–213.

263 *Aramco v. Saudi Arabia* (Arbitration Tribunal) (1958) 27 *ILR* 117, para. 27.

264 E. Somers, Inleiding tot het Internationaal Zeerecht (Kluwer Mechelen 2004) 36.

coastal ports but this approach depends heavily on reciprocity thus cancelling the notion of an absolute right of access to any coastal port.[265]

The quest for an absolute right to disembark can however be found in the situation of vessels in distress whose legitimacy must be based on a situation of bona fide emergency or force majeure, rather than a situation of improvisation and opportunism resulting from insufficient precaution at the beginning of the journey. In line with the theme of this work to defend migrants at sea, it is imperative to determine whether a ship carrying persons rescued at sea can be seen as a ship in distress. Most legal instruments on maritime law expressly avoid the definition of distress even SOLAS. SAR however presents the notion in phases:

> 10 – EMERGENCY PHASE: A generic term meaning, as the case may be, uncertainty phase, alert phase or distress phase;
> 11 – UNCERTAINTY PHASE: A situation wherein uncertainty exists as to the safety of a person, vessel or other craft;
> 12 – ALERT PHASE: A situation where apprehension exists as to the safety of a person, a vessel or other craft;
> 13 – DISTRESS PHASE: A situation where there is a reasonable certainty that a person, a vessel or other craft is threatened by grave and imminent danger and requires immediate assistance.[266]

The last phrase conjures scenarios that necessitate assistance such as the outbreak of an epidemy or the sea unworthiness of a vessel provoked by the large number of people it is carrying. SOLAS equally envisages a situation where a ship is rendered sea unworthy due to the rescue operations being carried out. It will however be odd to use the above reasons as justification for applying SOLAS rules on ships in distress.[267] Contrary to the above, the International Law Commission (ILC) posits that, when human life is at stake or where the physical integrity of a persons is being threatened, the ship is in distress. This conclusion is not limited to a few sick persons but equally to greater health threats to the crew and among persons rescued. This, according to the ILC, qualifies the ship as a ship in distress.[268]

265 Convention and Statute on the International Regime of Maritime Ports (adopted 9 December 1923, entered into force 26 July 1926) 515 *UNTS 350*.

266 Annex 1, Articles 1.3.10, 11, 12 SAR.

267 Article IV(b) SOLAS.

268 International Law Commission, Year book of the International Law Commission (ILC, New York, 1973) Vol. 11, 134, para. 4.

Still, it would be foolhardy to claim that a ship has the right to access a port without authorization because it is in distress. Given the relative reluctance by treaty law to grant any such rights to ships in distress, *stare decisis* relies heavily on the *Rebecca* case to conclude that a right of access to ships in distress does exist.[269] Certain academic legal opinion however holds contrary.[270] Other legal minds equally support this claim as a logical deduction from the existence of coastal sovereignty over internal waters and glaringly appear to be the preferred approach adopted by most coastal States.[271] This approach is buttressed by the Salvage Convention that grants the right for a coastal State to refuse the entry of a vessel in distress into its port when there is a risk (like pollution or terrorist attack) to that port.[272] In the same vein, SOLAS reiterates that a State has the right to decide who enters its ports even in emergency cases.[273]

Given the reluctance by States to cede parts of their sovereignty by accepting disembarkation duties, recent trends show an increase of interception operations even on the high seas in order to send back sea-borne migrants in contradiction to the principle of freedom of navigation that applies on the high seas.[274] It should however be noted that interception is permissible when the vessel to be intercepted flies no flag and in addition, certain interception measures against vessels are allowed when there are reasonable grounds to suspect the vessels of carrying out criminal activities like human trafficking and smuggling of migrants.[275]

Unfortunately, the highly malleable legal framework to combat trafficking in human beings and the smuggling of migrants has become an apt pretext to divert and return migrants, without any identification of potential asylum seekers or refugees in the context of mixed migration flows. Again, the interception of seaborne migrants in the territorial waters and contiguous zone can be justified by violations of local immigration laws and regulations. Despite the inherent need for proportionality in the exercise of these powers and the management of infractions, most States tend to abuse their powers in the management of these issues thus requiring better legislation.

---

269 Rebecca Case (Kate A. Hoff v. United Mexican States) (Mexico/USA General Claims Commission) (1929) 33 *American Journal of International Law* 860–860.

270 E. Somers, *Inleiding tot het Internationaal Zeerecht* (Kluwer Mechelen 2004) 38–40.

271 *See* Jasmine Coppens & Eduard Somers, 'Towards New Rules on Disembarkation of Persons Rescued at Sea?' (2010) 25(3) *The International Journal of Marine and Coastal Law* 377–403.

272 Article 11 of the Salvage Convention.

273 Article V(b) SOLAS.

274 Article 87(1) UNCLOS.

275 Article 110 UNCLOS.

The disembarkation dilemma has certainly had a negative impact on the provision of a safe place for distressed migrants due partly to non-legal considerations besides the legislative loopholes. A plausible answer to the non-legal considerations is the old approach of linking the disembarkation duty to financial arrangements or burden-sharing agreements that will be in line with the UNHCR principles of burden and responsibility sharing.[276] This approach will no doubt need major adaptations nowadays given the drastic change of destination by migrants who target developing countries unlike the Vietnamese boat people of the 1980s whose destinations were limited to neighbouring States who were not necessarily developed so they could count on the support of developing countries. Secondly, security concerns have a major preoccupation for most States nowadays. After major attacks like the 9/11, most States began to perceive migrants as serious sources of insecurity. It therefore becomes logical to either halt or redirect the flow of migrants in order to guarantee security rather than receive and integrate migrants after scrutiny.

Adaptations to these modern challenges can include capacity-building, as well as the creation of processing and reception centres. The European Union has already taken the lead by funding projects to improve the capacities of its member States so they can effectively deal with large groups of arrivals of irregular migrants like that of Lampedusa. Likewise, the communication on strengthened practical cooperation was issued by the commission in 2006, setting up rapid reaction units that could respond to sudden influxes of irregular migrants more effectively.[277] It is equally not out of place to use the burden sharing agreements as motivation for States to engage in resettlement and readmission agreements. This is simply because States will be more ready to accept disembarkation duties if they are certain that the burdens of disembarkation will be shared.

Another equally daunting task is that of attributing the duty of disembarkation to a State. This task rages with a delicate decision to make between the nearest port and the State responsible for the search and rescue. To this effect, a few basic tasks like imposing the duty to disembark, clearly defining the place of safety that should be binding and ensuring compliance with the principle of non-refoulement. The above intellectual tasks should ultimately

276 UNHCR EXCOM Conclusion No. 22 (XXXII) 'Protection of Asylum-Seekers in Situation of Large-Scale Influx' (1981), UNHCR EXCOM Conclusion No. 38 (XXXVI) 'Rescue of Asylum-Seekers in Distress at Sea' (1985).

277 Commission (EC), 'Strengthened practical cooperation' (Communication) COM (2006) 67 final, 17 February 2006.

link the duty to disembark with the duty to rescue and provision of a place of safety, thus encouraging the ratification of the SAR and SOLAS Amendments.

The new Law of the Sea Guidelines recently adopted by the European Parliament propose that priority of disembarkation should be granted to the third country from where the ship carrying the persons departed or through whose territorial waters or rescue region the ship transited. If this proves to be impossible, disembarkation priorities should go to the host member State, unless it is necessary to act otherwise to ensure the safety of the rescued persons.[278] This simply implies that the host country of the joint operation at sea carries the responsibility. This position is not shared by most States so the closest port remains the best option.

The disembarkation of persons in general and irregular migrants in particular remains an elusive legal issue given the absence of any binding legal obligation to grant these people access to their territory. In fact, the current situation can only be changed by States abandoning part of their sovereignty which they are not ready to do just yet. The dilemma has been transferred from one institution or agency to another with no definite solution and even deciding at some stage it was a regional issue not requiring any international legislation. Despite the need to insist on the implementation of the existing rules, it will be stupid to deny that the existing legal framework is in dire need of amendments. As a follow up, linking the duty to disembark need not necessarily be linked to the duty to rescue due to costs. The closest port should therefore be considered as a place of safety for both seafarers and those rescued at sea.

Part 4: The Cardinal Principle of Non-refoulement and the Legality of Interceptions

The phenomenon of 'boat people' sparked by the Indochinese crisis provoked deep reflections on how to deal with the arrival of overpopulated vessels to neighbouring States. The international community helplessly observed and was coerced to acknowledge and admit the existence of loopholes in

278 European Commission, Proposal for a Council Decision supplementing the Schengen Borders Code as regards the surveillance of the sea external borders in the context of the operational cooperation coordinated by the European Agency for the Management of Operational Cooperation at the External Borders, COM (2009) 658 final; and Council Decision of 26 April 2010 supplementing the Schengen Borders Code as regards the surveillance of the sea external borders in the context of the operational cooperation coordinated by the European Agency for the Management of Operational Cooperation at the External Borders, O.J. L 111/20 (4 May 2010).

international legislation dealing with such issues.[279] Indeed, the Gordian knot of the issue has remained unchanged over the years, comprising reconciling the humanitarian plight of refugees and asylum seekers with the Destination State's concerns about illegal immigration, mass migrations of people and the costs of asylum. This dilemma highlights the tension created between competing legal norms and between moral and legal norms.[280] It therefore becomes pivotal to examine the legal obligations incumbent upon coastal States and flag States in respect of asylum seekers rescued at sea.

Despite the presence of refugees in dire need of protection, sea-borne migration has always been considered by destination States as a burden. It has become trendy for States to deny refugee status to sea-borne migrants and even conjure security concerns to deny protection and justify the non-admittance or even removal of migrants. The overwhelming arrival of sea-borne migrants poses serious interpretation and application challenges to the principle of non-refoulement and the right to asylum as well as the related rules of freedom and safety of navigation.

Besides the legal challenges of identifying the rights and obligations of the concerned States in the different maritime zones in relation to search and rescue operations at sea, the principle of non-refoulement challenges the legal limits of the decision of States to refuse the permission of entry into their territories. The impactful role of the principle of non-refoulement in the protection of sea-borne migrants will therefore be examined from three angles namely its nature and status, practical application and finally challenges in naval operations.

4.1 *Legal Nature of the Principle of Non-refoulement*

The principle that a person cannot be sent, deported, extradited or transferred to a country where he or she faces a serious risk of torture or cruel, inhuman or degrading treatment is fundamental in human rights law. The application of this fundamental principle can however face serious challenges depending on the place of application. The case of refoulement at sea, which is our principal concern here, poses a unique problem. Refoulement at sea can be synonymous to a death sentence given the hostile natural conditions. Despite the quasi certainty of death in case of refoulement at sea, numerous actors still find subtle ways of circumventing their legal obligations to assist and bring to a place of

279 Seline Trevisanut, 'The Principle of Non-Refoulement at Sea and the Effectiveness of Asylum Protection' (2008) 12 *Max Planck Y.B. U.N. L.* 205, 246.

280 Richard Barnes, 'Refugee Law at Sea' (2004) 53(1) *International and Comparative Law Quarterly* 47–58.

safety. This is done by biased legal interpretations and the implementation of domestic policies which either reject migrants in distress or discriminate against some of them through selective entry rules thus exposing them to danger. It is therefore very important to ascertain the nature of this principle so to ensure the protection of such migrants in distress at sea.

4.1.1 Connotation of the Principle of Non-refoulement

As enshrined in Article 33(1) of the 1951 Refugee Convention, the principle of non-refoulement is sculpted in the following words: "No contracting State shall expel or return ('refouler') a refugee in any manner whatsoever to the frontiers of territories where his life or freedom would be threatened on account of his race, religion, nationality, membership of a particular social group or political opinion". This Article establishes an unequivocal obligation for States not to expulse individuals or groups of persons present in their territory to the State of persecution. A panoramic analysis of this Article highlights two major worries, namely who does the principle of non-refoulement protect and secondly, when precisely does rejection amount to a violation of the obligation of non-refoulement?

Despite the fundamental status of the principle of non-refoulement that literally guarantees the protection of asylum seekers,[281] it curiously falls short of assuring access into the territory of the State of destination or admission to the procedures granting the refugee status. Notwithstanding attempts by certain schools of legal thought to argue into existence such an additional obligation for States to grant such or admit asylum seekers into their territories, State practice to date still adopts a reticent stance.[282] Others have even adopted a more evolutionary definition of the principle of non-refoulement claiming to flow from the spirit of Article 33 of the 1951 Refugee Convention: 'Non-refoulement is about being admitted into the State community, although in a minimalist form of non-removal. It could be described as a right to transgress an administrative border'.[283]

Such a daring definition definitely carries heavy legal effects on border controls and the specific delimitations of areas of intervention. As will be later seen, the understanding of 'non rejection at the frontier' is quite blurred when

281 Sir Elihu Lauterpacht and Daniel Bethlehem, 'The Scope and Content of the Principle of *Non-Refoulement*: Opinion', in Erika Feller, Volker Türk and Frances Nicholson (eds.), *Refugee Protection in International Law* (Cambridge University Press 2003) 87, 107.

282 Guy S. Goodwin-Gill, Jane McAdam, *The Refugee in International Law* (3rd edition Oxford University Press 2007) 257 et seq.; and James C. Hathaway, *The Rights of Refugees under International Law* (Cambridge University Press 2005) 370 et seq.

283 Gregor Noll, 'Seeking Asylum at Embassies: A right to Entry under International Law?' (2005) 17 *International Journal of Refugee Law* 542, 548.

applied to the territorial waters or high seas because it becomes quite difficult to determine the moment of entry into the territory for sea-borne migrants. Whatever the case, the unlawful entry of sea-borne asylum seekers does not exclude them from the scope of application of the principle of non-refoulement as intended by the 1951 Refugee Convention:

> The contracting States shall not impose penalties, on account of their illegal entry or presence, on refugees who, coming directly from a territory where their life or freedom was threatened in the sense of article 1, enter or are present in their territory without authorization, provided they present themselves without delay to the authorities and show good cause for their illegal entry or presence.[284]

The above commitment by the 1951 Refugee Convention to protect refugees who travel to a State Party without authorization is probably the most pivotal novelty yet and deserves academic endorsement.[285] Very recent archives even show similar trends adopted by the UNHCR Executive Committee during the Indo-Chinese crisis:

> It is therefore imperative to ensure that asylum seekers are fully protected in large-scale influx situations, to reaffirm the basic minimum standards for their treatment ... In situations of large-scale influx, asylum seekers should be admitted to the State in which they first seek refuge and if that State is unable to admit them on a durable basis, it should always admit them at least on a temporal basis ... In all cases, the fundamental principle of non-refoulement, including non-rejection at the frontier must be scrupulously observed.[286]

The irrefutable importance of the principle of non-refoulement saw its subsequent inclusion into other respectable legal instruments like the 1967 Declaration on Territorial Asylum (DTA)[287] and the 1967 OAU Convention on Refugees,[288] which have proven indispensable for the interpretation for the 1951 Refugee Convention. This same importance pushed the Executive

284 Article 1 of the 1951 Refugee Convention.

285 C. Hathaway, 'Why Refugee Law Still Matters' (2007) 8 *Melbourne Journal of International Law* 89, 91.

286 Executive Committee, Conclusion No. 22 (XXXII) 1981; reaffirmed during the crisis in former Yugoslavia, in Executive Committee, Conclusion No. 74 (XLV) 1994, para. (r).

287 A/RES/2312 (XXII) of 14 December 1967.

288 OAU Convention Governing the Specific Aspects of Refugee Problems in Africa, UNTS Vol. 1001 No. 14691.

Committee reiterate the argument in 1979 during its sitting on migration by sea: "It is the humanitarian obligation of all coastal States to allow vessels in distress to seek haven in their waters and to grant asylum, or at least temporary refuge, to persons on board wishing to seek asylum".[289]

The mammoth role played by the UNHCR in the evolution of the principle of non-refoulement to include cases of rejection at the frontier as well broaden the interpretation of Article 33 in relation to the category of individuals protected cannot be undermined. The *rationae personae* application of the 1951 Refugee Convention as well as the mandate of the UNHCR portrays traces of incongruity. In fact, the scope of the mandate has progressively evolved to now comprise five categories including those defined by the 1951 Refugee Convention and the 1967 Protocol, those recognized by States as entitled to protection and assistance from the UNHCR, individuals who have benefited from the 'good offices' of the UNHCR, returning refugees and finally non-refugee stateless persons.[290] Article 33 of the 1951 Refugee Convention on the other hand applies to 'statutory refugees' or more simply put, individuals identified by Article 1 of the same Convention, as modified by the 1967 Protocol relating the Status of Refugees.[291]

Given the ambiguity inherent to the definition of refugee, Article 1 of the 1951 Refugee Convention unequivocally defined the term in the following words:

> The term refugee shall apply to any person who owing to well-founded fear of being persecuted for reason of race, religion, nationality, membership of a particular social group or opinion, is outside the country of his nationality and is unable or, owing to such fear, is unwilling to avail himself of the protection of that country; or who, not having a nationality and being outside the country of his former habitual residence as a result of such events, is unable or, owing to such fear, is unwilling to return to it.

The notion of 'well-founded fear' finely delimits the ambits of application of the Convention as compared to the mandate of the UNHCR. Another equally ambiguous subject has been the meaning of persecution. Scholarly attempts

289 Executive Committee, Conclusion No. 15 (XXX) 1979, para. (c).

290 UNHCR Protection of Persons – Concern to UNHCR Who Falls Outside the 1951 Convention: A Discussion Note, 2 April 1992, Doc. EC/1992/SCP.CRP.5, para. 11.

291 *Protocol relating to the Status of Refugees*, UNTS Vol. 606 No. 8791, page 267 et seq.; and the 1967 Protocol eliminated the limits of time and place in respect of the application of the 1951 Refugee Convention, which formerly applied only to refugees stemming from Europe because of events occurred before the 1 January 1951.

to widen the scope of the term are multifarious. Victims of armed conflicts and generalized violence normally received a favourable conclusion since any involuntary return to their country of origin will definitely expose them to danger.[292] Besides the above attempts, the notion of 'de facto refugees'[293] has been forged and public opinion holds that they are not deprived of the protection offered by the principle of non-refoulement as provided by the 'complementary protection' enshrined in human rights law.

Without necessarily examining the causes of migration, which may be human rights related or economic as the case usually is with migrants at sea, the UDHR clearly inscribes that '[e]veryone has the right to leave any country, including his own, and to return to his country[294] .... and everyone has the right to seek and enjoy in other countries asylum from persecution'.[295] The above articles grant the right for any human to flee danger from any risk zone to a place of safety but fail to guarantee any entry into any chosen State of destination that has the discretionary power to either accept or reject any request to enter its territory.[296] Notwithstanding the discretion of States, obstructing an individual from presenting a request can imply a breach of Article 14(1) UDHR that enshrines the notion of 'right to request' which is in turn safeguarded by the principle of non-refoulement. Besides the UDHR, the principle of non-refoulement has enjoyed enviable recognition by numerous other international legal instruments. Some of these include amongst others; Article 3 of the Convention against Torture, and other Cruel, Inhuman or Degrading Treatment or Punishment that forbids the removal of individuals to States where they risk being subjected to torture or other inhuman and

292 Goodwin-Gill *supra* note 279. Lauterpacht and Bethlehem have argued that the notion of threat contemplated in Article 33(1) of the Refugee Convention may be 'broader than simply the risk of persecution, [...] to the extent that a threat to life or freedom that may arise other than in consequence of persecution', enlarging thus the scope of Article 33 to refugees not included in the treaty definition of Article 1', *see* Lauterpacht, *supra* note 179.

293 'Persons not recognized as refugees within the meaning of Article 1 of the Refugee Convention and who are unable or unwilling for political, racial, religious or other valid reasons to return to their countries of origin', *see* Council of Europe Parliamentary Assembly Recommendation No. 773 (1976) on the Situation of *de facto* Refugees, para. 1.

294 Article 13(2) UDHR.

295 Article 14(1) UDHR.

296 M. Pallis, 'Obligations of States towards Asylum Seeker at Sea: Interactions and Conflicts Between Legal Regimes' (2002) 14 *International Journal of Refugee Law* 329, 341.

degrading treatment[297] while the ICCPR equally enshrines this same principle in its Article 7.[298]

A handful of regional legislative efforts also endorse the non-refoulement principle like Article 3 ECHR,[299] Article 22(8) of the 1969 American Convention on Human Rights,[300] Article 5 of the 1981 African Charter on the Protection of Human and Peoples' Rights (Banjul Charter),[301] Article 45 of the 1949 Fourth Geneva Convention on the Protection of Civilian Persons in Time of War and finally the ICCPR that expressly creates an obligation on parties not to extradite, deport, expel or return an individual to a country where there are well founded suspicions concerning a risk of irreparable harm to the right to life as sculpted in its Article 6.[302]

The above citations provide ample proof that the principle of non-refoulement is consecrated by three branches on international law, humanitarian law, human rights and refugee protection, which may overlap but evolve in smooth interaction for a more efficient protection of refugees in general and sea-borne migrants in particular. With the respectable acknowledgement of treaty law alongside positive academic opinion[303] and even more encouraging, contemporary practice,[304] it would not be out of place to say that the principle of non-refoulement is consensually drifting towards a status of customary norm, despite the lack of uniformity in its contents and scope.

4.1.2 Status of the Principle of Non-refoulement

While certain actors in the international scene lean on security threats to defend their caution and even reticence as to fully adopting and implementing the principle of non-refoulement, audacious scholars of international law

297 A/RES/39/46 of 10 December 1984.

298 Human Rights Committee, General Comment No. 20 (1992), Doc. HRI/HEN/1/Rev.1 of 28 July 1994, para. 9.

299 UNTS Vol. 213 No. 2886.

300 UNTS Vol. 1144 No. 17955.

301 1981 African Charter on the Protection of Human and Peoples' Rights (Banjul Charter) (1982) 21 *International Legal Materials* 58 et seq.

302 M. Nowak, U.N. Covenant on Civil and Political Rights: CCPR a Commentary (2nd edition 2005) 186.

303 Goodwin-Gill *supra*, footnote 85, 289.

304 Council Directive 2001/55/EC of 20 July 2001 on Minimum Standards for Giving Temporary Protection in the Event of A Mass Influx of Displaced Persons and on Measures Promoting a Balance of Efforts between Member States in Receiving Such Persons and Bearing the Consequences thereof, OJEC No. 212/12 of 7 August 2001.

like Allain have already knighted the principle to the rank of '*jus cogens*'.[305] The problem of the status of the principle is not a recent one. The Indochinese crisis of the 1970s witnessed a slight reticence of the principle by receiving countries like Malaysia, Singapore and Thailand who raised security exceptions as stated Article 33(2) of the 1951 Refugee Convention:

> The benefit of the present provision may not, however, be claimed by a refugee whom there are reasonable grounds for regarding as a danger to the security of the country in which he is, or who, having been convicted by a final judgement of a particularly serious crime, constitutes a danger to the community of that country.

It should however be noted that none of the concerned countries contested the application of the principle. In fact, the UNHCR observed that States:

> Overwhelmingly indicated that they accept the principle of non-refoulement as binding, as demonstrated, inter alia, in numerous instances where States have responded to UNHCR's representations by providing explanations or justifications of cases of actual or intended refoulement, thus implicitly confirming their acceptance of the principle.[306]

In addition to the above efforts, efforts antecedent to Allain's jus cogens position can be traced to 1982 where the peremptory nature of the non-refoulement principle was affirmed in conclusion 25 (XXXIII) of the Advisory Opinion on the Extraterritorial Application of Non-Refoulement Obligations under the 1951 Convention. The Executive Committee of the UNHCR made a step far beyond the state of the art at the time. States were requested to shun actions resulting in refoulement situations which would be 'contrary to fundamental prohibitions against these practices'.[307] The pivotal nature of the stakes enjoined the stake-holders to reaffirm the principle in more imperial terms stating:

> Distressed at the widespread violations of the principle of non-refoulement and of the rights of refugees, in some cases resulting in

305 J. Allain, 'The jus cogens nature of non-refoulement' (2001) 13 *International Journal of Refugee Law* 533, 545.

306 UNCHR, Advisory Opinion on the Extraterritorial Application of Non-Refoulement Obligations under the 1951 Convention relating to the Status of Refugees and its 1967 Protocol, 26 January 2007, para. 15.

307 Executive Committee, Conclusion No. 55 (XL), 1989, para. (d).

> loss of refugee lives, and seriously disturbed at reports indicating that large numbers of refugees and asylum seekers have been refouled and expelled in highly dangerous situations; recalls that the principle of non-refoulement is not subject to derogation.[308]

The 9/11 terrorist attacks inspired an even more detailed perception of the principle especially from the security perspective. The UN Security Council even adopted measures aimed at repressing the funding and the preparation terrorist attacks. Appropriate measures in conformity with international law were unavoidable prior to granting refugee status. Also, refugee status should not be abused to ease terrorist acts even if political motivations are not recognized as grounds for denying requests for extradition of alleged terrorists.[309]

As deduced by Allain, the legal vacuum in the definition of terrorism gives the States the latitude to determine the seriousness and culprits of the terrorism crime pursuant to Article 33(2) of the 1951 Refugee Convention, permitting the State to expel or extradite the concerned even back to their place of origin where their live is threatened. The UNHCR expressed concerns about the exclusion clauses adopted by certain States on a collective rather than on individual basis thus trampling on the individual nature of the right to seek asylum.[310]

From the above, it can be deduced that the acquisition of a peremptory status for the principle of non-refoulement still has a challenging route to cover as opined by other scholars who question the ambivalence of international actors and States' attitude towards the principle of non-refoulement. Doctrine[311] proposes an outlet to this ambivalence by suggesting that 'doubtful wording of the council's resolution must always be construed in such a way as to avoid conflict with fundamental international obligations'.[312] This suggestion appears particular handy when faced with security justifications for violating non-refoulement like the uncertain definition of terrorism that may distort the essence of Article 1F(b) of the 1951 Refugee Convention.

Although less timorous actors of the international scene like Swiss had confidently declared the peremptory nature of the principle of non-refoulement

308 Executive Committee, Conclusion No. 79 (XLVII), 1996, para. (i).

309 UN Security Council Resolution as/res/1373.

310 UNHCR, Note on the Impact of Security Council resolution 1624 (2005) on the Application of Exclusion under Article 1F of the 1951 Refugee Convention.

311 R. Bruin and K. Wouters, 'Terrorism and the Non-derogability of *Non-refoulement*' (2003) *International Journal of Refugee Law* 15.

312 A. Orakhelashvili, 'The Impact of Peremptory Norms on the Interpretation and Application of the United Nations Security Council Resolutions' (2005) 16 *EJIL* 59, 64, 80.

since 1985,[313] the state of the art still demands further clarifications for the peremptory nature to be fully established. Meantime, the principle remains and important tool for guaranteeing the well-organized prohibition of torture and the protection of fundamental rights. This justifies the extreme importance in determining the place, circumstances and procedures under which sea-borne migrants are entitled to this critical protection.

4.2 *Application of Non-refoulement on Maritime Frontiers*

The sovereignty of a coastal State extends beyond its land territorial and internal waters, and in the case of an archipelagic State, its archipelagic waters, to an adjacent belt of sea, described as the territorial sea[314] that cannot exceed 12 nautical miles as stated in Article 3 UNCLOS. The most heralded exception to this rule is without doubt the right of innocent passage enshrined in Article 17 UNCLOS. However, Articles 21(1) and 25(3) UNCLOS outline conditions under which the right of innocent passage can be denied. It is therefore pivotal to distinguish the kinds of operations carried out by the coastal States in their territorial waters. If the operations are aimed at the expulsion of the vessel, this should be exercised within the powers of the coastal State to expel vessels or persons it considers having unlawfully entered into territory, namely territorial sea.

UNCLOS recognizes implicitly that a vessel entering into a coastal State territory is thus subject to its jurisdiction. It therefore logically follows that the occupants of the vessel enjoy the rights guaranteed by the international obligations binding the interested State in respect to the persons submitted to its jurisdiction, amongst which is the principle of non-refoulement. More precisely, Article 31 of the 1951 Refugee Convention is applicable to cases guaranteeing immunity from penalties from refugees who have entered unlawfully into the asylum State. On the other hand, if the intervention of the asylum solely seeks to deny entry, this technically shifts the frontier to the area where the operation takes place. The concerned individuals are not yet under its jurisdiction, so state authorities are only limited by the principle of non-refoulement within its meaning of non-rejection at the frontier.[315]

313 D. Shelton, 'Normative Hierarchy in International Law' (2006) 100 *American Journal of International Law* 291, 316.

314 Article 2(1) UNCLOS.

315 The United States has adopted the WET FOOT/DRY FOOT policy which states that 'if they (sea-borne migrants) touch the US soil, bridges, piers or rocks, they are subject to US immigration processes for removal. If they are wet feet, they are eligible for return by the Coast Guard in accordance with Executive Order 12807', US Coast Guard, 'Alien Migrant Interdiction', as reported in Stephen Legomsky, Immigration and Refugee Law

The above policy is a crystal-clear example of the non-entry mechanisms aimed at denying access to the territory through the non-authorization of entry or through the creation of international zones in which neither domestic nor international law applies. There is equally the 'territorial excision' applied on seaborne asylum seekers by the Australian authorities that greatly inconveniences the comprehension of refoulement to a frontier, causing someone to remain on the same side of the frontier as they began yet not returned to any frontier. The principle of non-refoulement therefore suffers violation through attitudes like refusal of entry into the territorial sea and denial of access into the port of disembarkation.

4.2.1 Refusal of Entry into the Territorial Sea

The technical similarities between Article 29 of the Vienna Convention on the Law of Treaties of 1969 and Article 33 of the 1951 Refugee Convention are quite visible to State parties' territory including the territorial sea. Article 33 prohibits refoulement to 'the frontiers of territories where his life or freedom would be threatened'. The part of the territory concerned immediately loses its importance with the use of the word territory in its plural form. This interpretation can equally be applied to the states with jurisdiction over the territory that constitutes a danger to the life and freedom of the asylum seeker if he were to be refouled thereto.[316]

Mindful of the notion of 'territorial asylum',[317] the first State of arrival has the duty to host refugees at least temporarily. The vessel transporting refugees cannot be stopped from entering into the territorial sea upon its arrival at the border, neither can it be refouled to the high seas or territories where the risks of persecution are palpable. Despite its archaic origins from the Indochinese crises that sought a minimum standard of protection and a first hosting place, the notion of territorial asylum can be likened to today's idea of temporary refuge. In fact, the socio-economic burdens incumbent on the coastal States to shelter refugees and avoid refoulement after determining their status gave birth to the notion of a safe third State after the conclusion of agreements to this effect.

Despite the temporal refuge rule, states still morbidly deny access into their territorial waters pretexting the inexistence of proof of the presence of

---

and Procedure (4th edition) 684, footnote 44. United States President Executive Order No. 12.807, the 'Kennebunkport Order', authorised US authorities to interdict Haitian vessels on the high seas and to redirect them directly to Haiti.

316 European Court of Human Rights, *T.I. v. United Kingdom*, Appeal. 43844/98, Decision on the Admissibility, 7 March 2000, 15–16.

317 Declaration on Territorial Asylum, A/RES/2312 (XXII) of 14 December 1967.

refugees on board, glaringly hurting immigration law.[318] The legal arguments for the *Tampa* case are worth mentioning. Norway, the flag State of the Tampa, claimed the right of innocent passage had been violated by Australia which refused entry into its internal waters thereby breaching its obligation not to hamper the innocent passage of a vessel as mentioned in Article 24(1) UNCLOS. Australia rebutted under Article 19(2) UNCLOS that justified such refusal should domestic law be violated and pursued with Article 25(1) UNCLOS which authorised the coastal State to 'take the necessary step in its territorial sea to prevent passage that is not innocent'.

As earlier mentioned, doctrine still harbours loopholes in determining whether the violation of the coastal domestic law effectively constitutes a threat to the peace and security of the coastal State. To this effect, Article 19(2) UNCLOS states that a violation of one of the enlisted sectors automatically implies a general security threat to the coastal State, thus justifying the denial and even closure of part of its territorial waters. In fact, Article 25(2) UNCLOS stipulates:

> In the case of ships proceeding to internal waters or a call at a port facility outside internal waters, the coastal State also has the right to take the necessary steps to prevent any breach of the conditions to which admission of those ships to internal waters or such a call is subject.

A strict interpretation of this provision logically justifies the actions of Australia which can be said to have acted rightfully by denying the right of passage to Tampa. However, Australia's decision to redirect the vessel and outright refusal to carry out the preliminary screening of passengers can equally be interpreted as a violation of the principle of non-refoulement. It should be noted that the coastal State has the right to expel a vessel that has violated its domestic immigration law by entering its territorial seas thereby breaching the requirements for innocent passage. Obliging such a vessel to return to high seas equally constitutes a full right of the coastal State.

It would nevertheless be imprudent to regard such rights as unlimited. The application of such rights must fall within the ambits of international law obligations and in this particular case, the principle of non-refoulement. In the case of the Tampa, Australia chose New Zealand and Nauru which satisfied international standards in human rights and asylum law yet denied the passengers their intended destination which was Australia. Again, Australia as

318 Two cases illustrate this issue namely, the Norwegian Vessel TAMPA involving Australia, and the German Vessel CAP ANAMUR involving Italy.

first country of arrival, had the duty of temporary refuge and first screening of asylum requests that they failed to carry out.

The transfer of refugees to a safe third state for the final determination of the Status and subsequent repelling of ineligible refugees could have been justified only if the preliminary checks had been carried out. Similarly, the *Cap Anamur* case highlights meaning of entry in the jurisdiction of the coastal State that may come through an authorization granting admission to the port waters or by disembarkation. This line of defence obviously is non-applicable to vessels involved in smuggling migrants as well as vessels that subtly mask the exact moment of their entry and disembarkation.

4.2.2 Refusal of Disembarkation and Access to Ports

It should be noted right from the start that the coastal State enjoys exclusive competence to grant or deny access to the territory to irregular passengers after carefully analysing the stakes of any such decision. The *Cap Anamur* and *Tampa* cases constitute classic practical examples of refusal of access to ports and of disembarkation of asylum seekers. In the above cases, the masters of the vessels were considered responsible for the passengers because they represented the legal authority on board. From experience, two major groups of refugees can be identified namely the irregular passengers or individuals intentionally rescued by the vessel, and the case of stowaways. Whatever the case, both can be considered as clandestine migrants in need of protection that seems lacking in international law thus needs elucidation.

Although it never entered into force, the Brussels Convention relating to Stowaways clearly defines a 'stowaway' in its Article 1 as 'Une personne qui, an un port quelconque ou en un lieu à sa proximité se dissimule dans un navire sans le consentement du propriétaire du navire et qui est à bord après que le navire a quitté ce port ou ce lieu'.[319] This can be translated to English as 'A person who, at any port or place near it, conceals himself in a ship without the consent of the owner of the ship and who is on board after the ship has left such port or place'.

The resounding silence of international law on the question of stowaways leaves the port State with no obligations in relation to the concerned. It is however not uncommon for the port state to oblige the master of the vessel to retain the stowaway on board. A logical interpretation of such retention would liken it to an arrest on board and even a technical refusal of disembarkation.

---

319 F. Payre, 'Les passagers clandestins' (1966) 14 *Annuaire du Droit Maritime et Océanique* 277, 286; and A. Goy, 'Le régime international du passager clandestin' (2001) 6 *Annuaire du Droit de la Mer* 169, 171.

The French tribunals however ruled on this difference in the case of *Ben Salem et Taznaret*.[320] The tribunal ruled that the tribunal acted within the ambits of its prerogatives but abused its authority by forcefully preventing disembarkation. The tribunal further underlined that the forceful refusal of disembarkation constituted a violation of the fundamental freedom of movement of the concerned even if they may have decided to stay on board and try their luck in the next port.[321]

Scholarly articles have pushed the reflection a little further by insisting that local authorities can oblige foreign ship captains to retain clandestine passengers, basing their decision exclusively on their domestic law.[322] In fact, denying disembarkation to stowaways does not exclude the possibility of redirecting the vessel to another destination, which decision is left to the discretion of the concerned captain. However, the coastal State can ensure that the new destination does not constitute any danger to the fleeing persons on board.

Logically, the refusal of disembarkation often leads to the redirection of the vessel, which should be a voluntary act. This is however not always the case with certain coastal States who decide to manage the redirection and ensure their refusal is not subtly breached and/or their responsibilities are not evoked to criticise their refusal of disembarkation as legally baseless thus departing from the humanitarian values greatly advocated. The *Tampa* case is a glaring example of this situation. In this case, the Australian jurisdiction justified an arbitral detention by claiming that most migrants on board who were asylum seekers, were under the total control of the Australian authorities.[323] The Federal Court of Australia deemed such detention unlawful and called for the immediate release of the 433 detained passengers of the Tampa with Justice North motivating his decision by the fact that the Australian authorities unilaterally decided the movement and destination of the detained persons to

320 The case concerned the refusal of disembarkation of two stowaways from Morocco in the port of Honfleur, from a vessel sailing under the Antiguan flag. The ship-owner of German nationality invoked a violation of his right of property as well as a violation of the fundamental freedom of movement of the two unlawful passengers on board. *See* Tribunal des conflits, 12 May 1997, *Préfet de police de Paris c. Tribunal de grande instance de Paris* (*Ben Salem et Taznaret* case), A.F.D.I. 44 (1998), 684; and *Revue Française de Droit Administratif* 1997, Vol. 1, 523 et seq.

321 J. Arrighi de Casanova, 'Les limites de la voie de fait (police des strangers et liberts individuelle)' (1997) 1 *Revue Française de Droit Administratif* 514.

322 G. Bastid-Burdeau, 'Migrations clandestines et droit de lamer', in *La meret son droit, Mélanges offerts à Laurent Lucchini et Jean-Pierre Quinéudec* (Paris 2003) 57, 64.

323 *Vadarlis v. Minister for Immigration and Multicultural Affairs and Others* (V 900 of 2001 FCA 1297) of 11 September 2001; and 'Refugees – Detention within Australian territorial sea – Pacific solution – Migration Act', *Austr. Yb. Int'lL.* 21 (2001) 263.

New Zealand and Nauru. The trial judges conveniently aligned with this decision stating that:

> Where complete control over people and their destiny is exercised by others it cannot be said that the opportunity offered by those others is a reasonable escape from the custody in which they were held. The custody simply continues in the form chosen by those detaining the people restrained (para. 17).

Although the above opinion was eventually dismissed by a plenary of the Federal Court,[324] it should be emphasised that Australia did not comply with its duty deriving from its 'first asylum' rule. Worth noting that this controversy arose because the Australian authorities failed to proceed with a preliminary screening of the passengers before resettling them to New Zealand and Nauru for the final determination of their status. Due to the de facto detention, the passengers were penalized for their unlawful entry into the Australian territorial waters that constitutes a breach of international law notably Article 31 of the 1951 Refugee Convention as well as their failure to fulfil their obligations in relation the safety of life at sea.

Given the quasi-certainty of ship owners, assisting migrants in distress at sea, that coastal States are most likely to reject their request for disembarkation, the trendy approach has been to forcefully disembark and face the consequences as was the case with Captain Carola Rackete in Italy which was in the media spotlight in the early months of 2019. The practical nature of this case deserves even more attention in this work given its pertinence to the theme at stake herein.

Carola Rackete, the Master of the MV Sea Watch 3, was arrested on the 29th of June 2019 by Italian authorities for aiding and abetting illegal immigration and for forcing her way into the port of Lampedusa despite being denied authorization to disembark and causing damage to a police speedboat that tried to block her entry. She was carrying on board forty rescued migrants and had waited in international waters outside of Lampedusa for seventeen days whilst many of the migrants' physical and mental conditions deteriorated.

---

324 *Ruddock and Others v. Vadarlis and Others* (2001) 66 A.L.D. 25 (V 1007 of 2001, FCA 1329) of 18 September 2001, para. 5, in which the Chief of Justice dissented on the admissibility of the appeal considering arbitrary the detention of the *Tampa* passengers. See also White, '(...) subsequent legal issues', *supra* note 150, footnotes 61, 254.

Rackete had warned the Italian authorities that she feared for the safety of her vessel and those on board, but the Italian authorities maintained their stance of refusing disembarkation.

The chronology of the events that constituted the background of the trial case are as follows.

- Carola Rackete, the Master of the MV Sea Watch 3, flying a Dutch flag, rescued 53 migrants in the Libyan SAR zone that was 47 nautical miles off the coast of Libya, after receiving notifications of a potential distress situation from a distance sea monitoring aircraft titled the 'COLIBRI'.
- After establishing contact with coordination centres in Italy, Malta, Holland and Libya, with the Libyan Coast Guard assuming the coordination of the SAR event, the Sea Watch 3 proceeded to rescue the people in danger after informing the other authorities.
- At the end of the rescue, the commander immediately tabled a request for a place of safety to the concerned States.
- Libya communicated an assigned place of safety but the Sea Watch 3 reported that Libya could not qualify as a safe haven thus requesting an alternative port for landing.
- The ship then headed north towards the safe harbour closest to the rescue position but was ordered by the Italian Ministry of Interior not to enter Italian waters as the possible entry would be prejudicial to public order thus rendering even passage very offensive.
- With the Italian and Maltese coasts being the closest safe harbours, the ship came to within 17 nautical miles of the Italian island of Lampedusa that was the first port on its course.
- The Sea Watch 3 reiterated their request for a place of safety while insisting on the vulnerable and delicate situation of the rescued persons. The Italian authorities however stuck to their domestic laws stating 'urgent provisions on the fight against illegal and orderly immigration and public security' amended my penal laws tightening the penalties for some criminal cases related to illegal immigration'. This argument was used to strengthen the prohibition of the Italian authorities.
- Meantime, the Italian authorities sent an inspection ship with medical inspectors to the Lampedusa station to ascertain the sanitary conditions of the migrants after which those in need were transferred to the island Harbour Master's Office by boat.
- Repeated subsequent requests from the sea to the Maritime Rescue Coordination Centre of the Harbour Offices, with medical reports attached stayed numb.

- The situation continued for a few more days before the Vedetta alongside a CP312 patrol boat were sent to halt the advancing Sea Watch 3 and ordered to leave the Italian waters in accordance with orders issued by the Italian authorities.
- The commander disregarded the orders and pursued her navigation towards the island of Lampedusa invoking necessity while requesting a place to moor inside the port of Lampedusa.
- Soldiers were sent to inquire more information about the immigrants on board and another migrant was evacuated for medical care.
- The police report aided the opening of a case file against the commander by Dr. Salvatore Vella, deputy prosecutor of the public prosecutor's office at the court of Agrigento.

The above facts which were related in simple media jargon for purposes of information, received a judicial classification to ease the imputation of charges. Thus, the judge for preliminary investigations, Dr. Alessandra Vella, of the Court of Agrigento, stated that:

> [A]fter having repeatedly received by order from the Guardia di Finanza by radio, the order to stop the motion – not being authorized to enter the port of Lampedusa – and having then been approached by the lookout V.808 of the Guardia di Finanza, with activation of the signals required by the International Code to desist from entering the port, undertaking evasive manoeuvres at the repeated alt orders imposed by the lookout, operating the on-board engines and directing the route to the port; then, after entering the port, he headed towards the quay of the commercial pier, already occupied by the look-out V.808 moored there with flashing lights and navigation lights turned on, until it hit the left side of the patrol boat with its own left side.[325]

The commander of the Sea Watch was charged with two crimes under Italian Code of Criminal Procedures namely Article 1100 for acts of resistance and violence against the warship Vedetta V.808 of the Guardia di Finanza, and Article 337, for the use of violence to oppose public officials on board the Guardia do Finanza V.808 while carrying out maritime police acts.

---

325 Court of Agrigento, Judge's Office for Preliminary Investigations, Order of Request of Validation of State and Duty of Application of the Measure, Article 391, in relation to Articles 272 et seq. Code of Criminal Procedure – the Judge of Preliminary Investigations, Dr. Ssa Alessandra Vella.

The Italian jurisdiction recognised the importance of examining the charges against Carola Rackete in the light of what preceded her actions, namely the rescue at sea and the obligations arising from it, in particular, the Constitutional Charter, the international conventions, the customary law and the General Principles of Law recognised by the United Nations, which place specific obligations both on the commanders of the ships and on the heads of the contracting States, with regards to rescue operations at sea. Based on the above premises, the underlying legal framework needed to be clarified. The court therefore lay down as follows:

> It should be said that, based on art. 10 of the Constitution, the Italian legal system conforms to generally recognized norms of international law. Among these are those set by the international agreements in force in Italy, which assume, on the basis of the fundamental principle *pacta-sunt-servanda*, a character of super-ordination with respect to the internal discipline pursuant to art. 117 of the Constitution, according to which legislative power is exercised in compliance, among other things, with the constraints deriving from international obligations.

The analysis here should begin with reference made to UNCLOS, ratified and enforced in Italy with Law 2 December 1994, n. 689, which constitutes a fundamental normative text on the subject of navigation law. Article 98 UNCLOS requires the commander of a ship to provide assistance to anyone in danger at sea and to go to the aid of people in difficulty as soon as possible if he is informed that such persons need assistance, within the limits of the reasonableness of the 'intervention. SOLAS signed in London in 1974 and enforced in Italy with the Law 2.3 of May 1980, nr. 313 (and subsequent amendments) also requires the ship's captain to provide assistance to people in danger. Next, SAR, enforced in Italy with the Law of 3 April, should be considered. SAR, concerning maritime search and rescue, is based on the principle of international cooperation and establishes that the allotment of the search and rescue areas must take place in agreement with the other States concerned. Based on the aforementioned legislation, the powers and duties of intervention and coordination on the part of the apparatuses of a single State in the area of competence do not exclude (in fact, in a certain sense they impose on the basis of the obligation above delineated) that naval units of different flags can begin the rescue when the imminent danger for human lives requires it.

The obligation of international law, incumbent on the master of a ship to proceed with the rescue (of the vessel and, when this is not possible, of the persons on board) finds, particularly in domestic law, a penal reinforcement in Article 1158 of the Navigation Code that punishes criminally the omission by the master of a ship, national or foreign, to lend assistance or grope the rescue in cases where there is the obligation pursuant to Article 490 of the same code, that is, when the ship in difficulty is completely incapable of performing the manoeuvres. In particular, this provision should be noted for the specific relevance it assumes with respect to the assessment of the lawfulness of the conduct of the suspect. As laid down in Article 18 UNCLOS and Article 10 of the Italian Legislative Decree 286/98, the first rule defines what must be understood as a harmless passage of a ship in the territorial sea:

> 'Passage' means navigation in the territorial sea for the purpose of:
> 1. cross it without entering inland waters or calling at a roadstead or port facility located outside of inland waters;
> 2. Head for inland waters or leave it, or stop at a harbour or port facility'.

From the above, the passage must be continuous and rapid. However, the passage allows the stop and the anchoring, but only if these constitute ordinary navigation events or are made necessary by force majeure or by difficult conditions, or are aimed at providing assistance to persons, ships or aircraft in danger.

The ensuing Article 19 foresees (bringing back the useful passage in the context in question): The passage is excusable as long as it does not prejudice the peace, good order and security of the coastal State. This transfer must be carried out in accordance with this Convention and other provisions of international law. In this light, the passage of a foreign ship is considered prejudicial to the peace, good order and security of the coastal State if, in the territorial sea, the ship is engaged in any of the following activities, including g) the loading or unloading of materials, currency or persons in violation of the laws, customs, fiscal, health or immigration regulations in force in the coastal State.

The above maritime, political and legal events led to the detention and arraignment of Carola Rackete for the above-mentioned crimes. It is worth noting that Rackete was later on released on bail and the charges were eventually dropped in 2021.[326] This temporal ruling however carries very interesting legal elements that can act as legal stepping stones in the protection of

326 DW, 'Italy drops Carola Rackete charges' (23 December 2021) <https://www.dw.com/en/italy-drops-charges-against-sea-watch-captain-carola-rackete/a-60245299> accessed 12 July 2023.

migrants in the seas. Without ignoring the arguments presented by the court for quashing the arrest, the most important justification given by the investigating magistrate stating that 'the conduct put up by Rackete, cannot be automatically examined, but must be examined uniformly and in the light of what precedes it, namely the rescue at sea and the obligations arising from it'.[327]

The failure of the preceding jurisdictions to consider this pivotal factor rendered their arrest decision contradictory, incorrect and inadequately reasoned. The Public Prosecutor further maintained that:

> In reviewing the notion of rescue ... it is possible to identify the notion of emergency assistance in an evaluation that is not in the abstract, but in practice .... rescue consists in the management of the stowaways in a place of safety, the adequacy of which must be assessed in relation to the materiality of the case.[328]

Another substantial precedence worth mentioning is the questioning by the prosecuting judge on the penalty to be paid for a conduct that consists of carrying rescues even in violation of legitimate and enforced national laws. Here, Judge Luigi refers to SAR stating that certain conditions must be observed to sanction such a conduct namely:

> 1-the safety of the threatened ship is no longer in danger;
> 2-primary needs (food, housing and medical care) are assured; and
> 3-transfer of stowaways to final destinations must be organised'.

This approach he justified by the fact that the 'supra-national law does not seem to be strictly related to a 'safe haven', but to the concept of 'safe place', not recognising in this concept an absolute and unequivocal meaning ...'. From this, the ugly legal and practical insufficiencies and uncertainties re-emerge especially with the weaknesses of the Guidelines for SAR and SOLAS claiming in para. 614 that 'the place of safety may be on land or it may be aboard to rescue until other suitable areas that can serve as place of safety if found or the rescued are disembarked in the next destination.' Judge Luigi draws the conclusion that for the identification of a place of safety, 'we do not necessarily need to refer to high land but may also be identified as such a place where

327 Prosecutor's Office, Agrigento Court, Application for Cassation, ATL 606 C.P.P., Public Ministries, Datt Luigi Patronaggio and Dr. Gloria Andreoli, Attorney of the republic of the Tribunal of Agrigento, 16th of July 2019.

328 *Ibid.*, note 2, page 14 of ruling of 16 July 2019.

primary assurance and temporary security are ensured up to the conduction of the vessel to the place of final landing'. However, the ruling insists that it would not be rational to exclude the unlawfulness of a conduct because it is enacted in fulfilment of a duty, without considering the intrinsic limits that follow this fulfilment as well as evaluating the overall assets that the legal system intends to protect. Rather than authorise and legalise the abandonment of migrants in distress at sea, this partial ruling encourages the respect of international duties within the ambits of the safety and security of the concerned parties. In fact, the assessment of the intrinsic values of each particular case needs to be considered before ruling on similar cases.

It would therefore be unwise for unscrupulous vessels to bank on this ruling to engage in unlawful activities but at the same time, the Court of Agrigento ruling acts as a moral and legal booster to timorous vessels who willingly abandon vessels in distress because of their fear of the reaction of the coastal States in relation to granting disembarkation and a place of safety.

Part 5: The Legality of Interceptions

Over the years, interception has progressively established itself as one of the most favourite anti-migration weapons by coastal States thanks to its flexibility to being able to be applied in multifarious contexts that satisfy numerous policy objectives.[329] The most common justifications for this use and abuse of the concept of interception include: law enforcement, combatting illegal migration, smuggling and/or trafficking activities, or even as a deterrent against the abuse of asylum laws. Occasionally, interception is even used to combat the irregular movement of refugees who have already secured protection in another country. It would be inequitable to side line the increasingly popular argument that interception is simply a migration management tool used to prevent undocumented migrants from crossing international waters. Prior to examining the aspects of interception that hinder the effective protection of migrants by sea, it is imperative to look at the connotations and denotations of interception as a concept.

According to Barbara Miltner, the accruing prevalence of interception is directly disproportional to its understanding given the degree of ambiguity and confusion that persists with regard to the exact meaning of the term.[330]

---

329 UNHCR, Perspectives from UNHCR and IOM, 10, EC/50/SC/CRP.17 (June 9, 2000).

330 Barbara Miltner, 'Irregular Maritime Migration-Refugee Protection issues in Rescue and Interception' (2006) 30(1) *Fordham Int'l L.J.* 75, 125.

This academic observation is buttressed by the litany of associated terminology used to imply, replace or explain interceptions.[331] Some of these terms include interdiction,[332] push-backs,[333] non-entrée[334] and even non-admission measures.[335] Most often, this multifarious terminology only serves to mask the true policies of the concerned States judged inappropriate by stake-holders. Given the biased interpretations that may carry broader or narrower connotations, it would be prudent to stick to the term 'interception', while providing a definition that should effectively protect migrants at sea. The phenomenon of interceptions therefore is analysed in three sections namely; meaning and practice, the issue of interception cloaked as rescue and finally the loopholes of the practice of interceptions.

5.1 *Meaning and Practice of Interception*

The ambiguity of interception both in theory and practice makes it a lethal weapon in the hands of States against migrants at sea. With the absence of a solid international legal regime applicable to extraterritorial anti-legal immigration operations, the fate of migrants at sea becomes even more uncertain. The uncertainty facilitates the abuse of rights and justifies numerous illegal operations which are biasedly carried out to the detriment of numerous migrants at sea. It is therefore pivotal to ascertain the practice and pave the way for a legal and practical application which should give greater and equal protection to migrants at sea regardless of their status.

5.1.1 Meaning of Interception

The most outstanding curiosity about the notion of interception is the absence of a universal definition. Notwithstanding, the most popular of the attempts is that proposed by the UNHCR which defines interception thus:

---

331 Andrew Brouwer & Judith Kumin, 'Interception and Asylum: When Migration Control and Human Rights Collide' (2003) 21 *Refuge* 6, 7.

332 Standard North American synonym for Interception, *see Sale v. Haitian Ctrs. Council Inc.*, 509 U.S. 155 (1993).

333 Despite its narrower meaning in the maritime context, it is interchangeably used with interception and tends to imply the specific practice of intercepting foreign vessels within territorial waters, and forcefully repelling it into the high seas thus preventing entry or disembarkation. Human Rights Watch, *Stemming the Flow: Abuses Against Migrants, Asylum Seekers and Refugees* (Sept. 2006).

334 James C. Hathaway, 'The Emerging Politics of Non-Entre' (1992) Refugees 40, 41.

335 Jens Vedsted-Hansen, Non-Admission Policies and the Right to Protection: Refugees Choice Versus States' Exclusion?, in Frances Nicholson & Patrick Twomey (eds.), *Refugee Rights and Realities: Evolving International Concepts and Regimes* (Cambridge University Press 1999) 269, 269–70.

> All measures applied by a State, outside its national territory, in order to prevent, interrupt, or stop the movement of persons without the required documentation crossing international boarders by land, air or sea, and making their way to the country of prospective destination.[336]

The extraterritorial character of interception as stated in this definition evidently carries heavy legal implications regarding State duties under international treaty law. For purposes of clarity, an extraterritorial act can generally be considered as any action that takes place either in the territory of another State or in international territory like the high seas.

Despite the contemporary pertinence of the extraterritorial notion in defining the concept of interceptions, the evolution of the domain further amendments to the definition barely three years later by the same UNHCR. In fact, the Executive Committee of the UNHCR redefined interception as one of the measures employed by States to:

> i. prevent embarkation of persons on an international journey;
> ii. prevent further onward international travel by persons who have commenced their journey; or
> iii. assert control of vessels where there are reasonable grounds to believe the vessel is transporting persons contrary to international or national maritime law;
>
> where, in relation to the above, the person or persons do not have the required documentation or valid permission to enter; and that such measures also serve to protect the lives and security of the traveling public as well as persons being smuggled or transported in an irregular manner.[337]

This second definition places emphasis of the State's intention to interrupt the movement of undocumented persons as well as introduces some other elements that deserve to be examined. The first most remarkable adjustment is the removal of the extraterritorial element that was enshrined by the first definition. The elimination of the extraterritorial notion was justified by the specificity of the maritime context wherein interceptions can occur in a State's territorial waters or in the high seas with contemporary State practice

---

336 UNHCR ExCom, Interception of Asylum Seekers and Refugees, The International Framework and Recommendations for a Comprehensive Approach, 10, EC/50/SC/CRP.17 (June 9, 2000).

337 UNHCR ExCom, Conclusion on Protection Safeguards in Interception Measures, No. 97 (LIV) (Oct. 10, 2003).

predominantly effecting high seas interceptions since States seek to exploit the legal ambiguities that flow from intercepting vessels further out at sea.[338] Despite the justification, practical trends suggest that it would be smart to continue using the extraterritorial notion.

One of the most imposing reasons for keeping the extraterritorial principle intact concerns the scope of interception[339] which covers a dramatically wider range of activities, including activities not traditionally perceived as interception.[340] The latest definition therefore muddies legal waters by failing to integrate the notion of extraterritoriality that better grasps the interceptions occurring on the high seas, involving extraterritorial disembarkation or processing or trapping asylum seekers and refugees within their State of origin.

Another noteworthy aspect of the ExCom definition is its explicit distinction between interception and rescue. The preamble italicises the fact that '[w]hen vessels respond to vessels in distress at sea, they are not engaged in interception'.[341] This constitutes a clear promotion of the highly desired humanitarian character of rescue as opposed to the migration control policy objectives that characterise interception practices. Despite this laudable effort, there is still a loud cry to clearly differentiate acts of rescue from acts of interception and clearly set out their boundaries.

It should be noted that the ExCom definition of interception simultaneously blurs the line between rescue and interception by suggesting that '[i]nterception also serves to protect the lives and security of the travelling public as well as persons being smuggled or transported in an irregular manner'.[342] Even though humanitarian objectives may be attained during the operation of the interception of trafficking victims or smuggled persons exposed to serious harm, it should be noted that the ultimate outcome of interception as

338 Bruce Finley, 'U.S. 'Extends Borders' to S. American Coasts' (Dec. 19, 2004) *Arizona Daily Star*, at A17 (citing a U.S. Department of Homeland Security policy of 'pushing our borders out' near the coast of Ecuador).

339 To prevent embarkation, prevent further onward international travel or assert the control of vessels in relation to those without proper documentation.

340 Activities such as detention within transit States often used for irregular migrants awaiting processing, hearings, deportation, or removal – would also be captured under the ExCom definition as well as preventing disembarkation from inside the intercepting State by imposing exit visas or border closures to prevent departure; and Concluding Observations of the Human Rights Committee: France, 20, U.N. Doc. CCPR/C/79/Add.80, Aug.4, 1997.

341 UNHCR ExCom, Conclusion No. 97, note 8.

342 *Supra*, note 12.

a common practice is not very clear.[343] Even if interception has a few humanitarian benefits, it can comfortably be said that migration concerns and security concerns constitute the principal motives behind the practice.

The International Organization for Migration actually observed that States that have the ability to do so find that intercepting migrants before they reach their territories is one of the most effective measures for enforcing their domestic migrations laws and policies.[344] The morbid intellectual practice of trying to portray interception as a humanitarian practice is not only ethically repugnant to the values of international law, but also contributes to clouding the clarity between interception and rescue. Lastly, the Excom definition talks of the physical interception of vessels when it mentions 'control of vessels' as opposed to the general reference to 'all measures' proposed by the previous definition of 2000. This seems to suggest that physical interception is important enough to be distinguished from administrative interception measures that may have unique characteristics.

5.1.2 Interception in Practice

The practice of interception can be considered as either physical or administrative in nature depending on the goals of the concerned State.[345] Administrative measures have significantly evolved in recent years due to the increase in migrants by sea. The administrative measures most often include a vast range of activities such as implementation of visa requirements, carrier solutions (for failure to detect and deter irregular migrants from entering the interdicting State), safe third country and country of first asylum determination or deflection, the posting of immigration officials in transit points to identify false documents and suspicious migrants and finally the training and posting of airline officials at overseas airports and other transit hubs to screen documents and migrants prior to boarding.[346] Administrative interception may equally include legislative action such as the creation of international zones or excised territories where more special immigration laws are implemented.[347]

---

343 Michael Pugh, 'Drowning Not Waving: Boat People and Humanitarianism at Sea' (2004) 17 *J. Refugee Stud.* 50, 62.

344 UNHCR Global Consultations on Int'l Protection, Refugee Protection and Migration Control: Perspectives from UNHCR and IOM 2, U.N. Doc. EC/GC/01/11 (May 31, 2001).

345 Stephen Legomsky, *Immigration and Refugee Law and Procedure* (4th ed. 2005) 1095–1135.

346 Barbara Miltner, 'Irregular Maritime Migration – Refugee Protection Issues in Rescue and Interception' (2006) 30 *Fordham Int'l L.J.* 75, 125.

347 Amuur v France, 19776/92 Eur. Ct. H.R. 25 (1996) (regarding France's 'international zone'). Australia remains a very good example on the creation of such international zones or excise territories especially with the Tampa case.

Physical interception on the other hand is more limited and mostly concerns the interference with vessels, usually in the maritime context, and may include the boarding, inspection, seizure, and/or destruction of vessels.[348] Other visible activities of physical interception may include push-backs in which boats intercepted in territorial waters may be forcibly escorted back out into the high seas to prevent disembarkation in the coastal State.[349] It is worth mentioning that physical interception is the main point of focus in the quest to protect migrants in the seas. The dire desire to protect migrants at sea has most often been weakened by the subtle use of interceptions as rescue missions. This situation deserves full examination given its importance to this work.

5.2 *Interception in the Veils of Rescue*

The UNHCR raised the concern as to veiled interceptions in the Mediterranean basin in 2006 pointing to 'the practice whereby several states were classifying some interception measures as rescue at sea operations, in order to use SAR operational capacity for such activities'.[350] As a result, this weakens the rescue regime and frustrates the distinction between rescue and interception. Consequently, delimiting the ambits of interception and rescue so to avoid an over lapse of attributes and possible abuse by stakeholders is vital. The problem of determining the exact moment when rescue becomes interception can be resolved by examining the underlying motives of State practice.

First and foremost, the simple fact that an action is termed a 'rescue' provides an instant legal basis to interfere with another vessel, especially on the high seas, where the limited 'right of visit' exceptions may be unavailable. In clearer terms, if a flag vessel is from another flag State, and not suspected of smuggling or piracy, interference is strictly forbidden unless expressly authorised by the flag State, unless it is in distress. Given the remote and unsupervised nature of the high seas alongside State pressure to intercept, rescue inevitably becomes a more logical justification for interference on the high seas.

Another plausible temptation for cloaking interceptions as rescue is the relative ease with which rescue vessels can be relieved of further responsibility after disembarkation. Given the amendments aimed at improving rescue disembarkations, veiled interceptions are likely to increase because a rescue operation on the high seas now affords prompt disembarkation coordinated

348 UNHCR ExCom, Interception of Asylum-Seekers and Refugees, *supra* note 15.

349 Robert L. Newmark, 'Note, Non-refoulement Run Afoul: The Questionable Legality of Extraterritorial Repatriation Programs' (1993) 71 *Wash. U. L. Q.* 833, 847.

350 State Representatives' Meeting on Rescue at Sea and Maritime Interception in the Mediterranean, Chairman's Summary, 1, 23–24, Madrid, May 2006.

by a third party, whereas a high seas interception affords no clear responsibilities in relation to protection of the disembarked migrants.

With the increasing tendency to endorse military vessels with the dual role of interception and rescue, it becomes difficult to determine the course of action for such vessels when they identify an unseaworthy boat under reasonable suspicion of smuggling. This dilemma exists because the unseaworthiness justifies rescue while the suspicion for smuggling credits interception. In fact, the response to this dilemma determines the disembarkation and protection responsibilities for those on board, given that the SAR and SOLAS amendments have created one disembarkation scheme for rescue victims, while the ExCom conclusion proposes a separate disembarkation scheme for intercepted persons.[351]

In 2005, the UNHCR ruminated on the 'range of concerns and objectives' motivating States to intercept.[352] One of the ambiguous factors motivating interception included 'the humanitarian imperative to come to the aid of those travelling in unseaworthy vessels … which constitutes an added element of interception practices'.[353] Curiously, the US Coast Guard adopted a similar position in its Alien Migrant Interdiction Program as involving 'primarily a humanitarian responsibility to prevent the loss of life at sea, since the majority of migrant vessels are dangerously overloaded, unseaworthy or otherwise unsafe.'[354] Such diction is ethically repugnant as it overtly equates interception with an underlying humanitarian-based rescue objective. This is simply because vessels responding to distressed persons at sea are clearly rescuing so cannot be equally mandated to intercept.

After ruminating on the deadlock for some time, the ExCom settled on the Conclusion document that holds in its preamble that 'when vessels respond to persons in distress, they are not engaged in interception.'[355] This technically means that distress must be ascertained before rescue can be claimed. This position seems comforting at first blush until confronted with marine terminology that always equates 'distress' to 'unseaworthiness' which is theoretically

351 UNHCR, Summary of Discussions, *supra* note 12.

352 UNHCR, Expert Roundtable on Rescue at Sea and Maritime Interception in the Mediterranean, Athens, Greece, Sept. 12–13, 2005, Background Discussion Paper, Reconciling Protection Concerns with Migration Objectives, Protection Policy & Legal Advice Section, at 7.

353 Ibid.

354 U.S. Coast Guard Office of Law Enforcement, Alien Migrant Interdiction: Introduction <https://www.pacificarea.uscg.mil/Our-Organization/District-11/Response-Division/LE/Migrants1/(accessed/> accessed 30 June 2023.

355 UNHCR ExCom, Conclusion No. 97, note 24.

inappropriate. The situation stays unresolved even with the addition of the non-binding clause that states that 'any encounter with a migrant vessel in distress should be characterised as rescue'.

The SAR definition of distress however sheds some light on the issue as it defines distress as a 'situation wherein there is a reasonable certainty that a person, a vessel or other craft is threatened by grave and imminent danger and requires immediate assistance.'[356] The drafting uses the phrase 'reasonable certainty' which should be differentiated from other phases characterised by uncertainty or apprehension as to the safety of the vessel.[357] In clearer terms, the unseaworthiness of a vessel is a matter of degree, and any good faith rescue operation must be justified by reasonable certainty of grave and imminent danger.

The trendy attitude of characterising interceptions as rescues is an ethically morbid act and legally detrimental position that undermines the rescue regime and overburdens coastal States with undue disembarkation duties. If it persists, persons in genuine need of international protection will be exposed to danger in the seas. The SAR definition therefore provides a solid departure point for distinguishing rescue from interception operations that can go a long way to curbing the abuse of the legal weaknesses examined herein below.

5.3 *Protection Loopholes in Interception*

The principal challenges posed by interception in the protection of migrants can be compressed under two main folders namely; identifying the State responsible for initial protection concerns in case of interception and, distinguishing intercepted refugees from those requiring international protection. This twin division is justified by the fact that numerous migrants intercepted especially during vast migration fluxes are usually returned to harm for lack of any uniform procedural standards in relation to screening.[358]

Sadly, there are presently no known international regulations governing disembarkation in the context of interception. Colossal efforts have however been deployed especially by the UNHCR to ameliorate refugee protection in this context. The recurring bottleneck to these efforts remains the tussle of interests between the international protection of migrants on the one hand and the promotion of State migration control tactics. These competing interests

356 Annex Chapter 1.3.13 SAR.

357 Chapters 1.3.11 & 1.3.12 SAR, respectively.

358 UN News Service, 'Refugees May Be Caught up in European Crackdown on Illegal Migrants' (2 February 2, 2005) <https://news.un.org/en/story/2005/02/127542> accessed 30 June 2023.

even concerned international organisations. By way of example, while the International Organisation for Migration upholds interception as 'one of the most effective measures to enforce domestic migration laws and policies', the UNHCR opines that 'one of the main challenges resulting from interception is the difficulty of reconciling this practice with relevant international legal responsibilities'.[359] These divergent perspectives have severely stifled protection efforts between both agencies.

With the ever-increasing justifications for interceptions to cover a wider scope, the UNHCR strove to incorporate protection safeguards into interception measures in order to prevent violations of refugee and human rights laws,[360] and eventually drafted protection guidelines on the subject.[361] Although the Executive Committee failed to effectively address numerous interception scenarios, it constituted a concrete advancement in the creation of a framework linking interception activities to protection duties for those intercepted.[362]

5.4 *Responsibility for Protection of Intercepted Persons*

An important observation is the fact that most of the recommendations made by the UNHCR ExCom *Conclusion on Protection Safeguards in Interception Measures* are already integrated into the Smuggling Protocol. This constitutes a veritable foundation for the eventual drafting of guidelines on refugee protection safeguards in interception measures despite the pressing need for more adapted measures. The ExCom Conclusion attributes State responsibility for intercepted persons thus; responsibility within sovereign territory, different territorial waters, contiguous zone and high seas, land-based interceptions.

5.4.1 Interception within Territorial Waters

It should first and foremost be reiterated that sovereignty in territorial waters is limited solely by innocent passage and this passage would not be considered innocent if the vessels seeking to disembark persons violates the domestic migrations laws of the coastal State. Since States use interception to assert control over vessels reasonably suspected of transporting persons contrary to

359 UNHCR Global Consultations on Int'l Protection, Refugee Protection and Migration Control: Perspectives from UNHCR and IOM 2, U.N. Doc. EC/GC/01/11 (May 31, 2001).

360 UNHCR's Global Consultations on International Protection was a forum convened in recognition of the fiftieth anniversary of the Refugee Convention, and the third track meetings were held within the framework of the Executive Committee to tackle issues not adequately covered by the Convention and interception was chosen as one of the main topics. *Also*, UNHCR, Update on Global Consultations on International Protection, 12–16.

361 Ibid., footnote 31.

362 UNHCR ExCom, Conclusion No. 97.

international and national maritime laws, the ExCom of the UNHCR proposed a very logical approach in relation to duties in the territorial waters.

To this effect, the intercepting State is responsible for providing the necessary protection safeguards for persons within its sovereign territory. States are therefore free to intercept vessels violating their domestic and international legislation so long as their interception does not result in the violation of any international legal commitments. With such interception, the intercepting state becomes responsible for protection needs like screening intercepted persons, preventing the return of those in need of international protection in violation of non-refoulement obligations.[363]

5.4.2 Interception in Foreign Territorial Waters

UNCLOS unequivocally states that the sovereignty of the coastal State extends, beyond its land territory and internal waters and, in the case of an archipelagic State, its archipelagic waters, to an adjacent belt of sea, described as the territorial sea.[364] As a result, any entry into this zone requires authorization if not done for purposes of innocent passage. In this scenario, the ExCom curiously attributes protection responsibilities to the passive State in whose zone the interception is being carried out and not to the State actively executing the interception. This strange decision gives the impression that the intercepting activities of one State impose responsibilities on another State.

This apparent anomaly is resolved by the fact that, as stated in Article 2(1) UNCLOS, no activity besides innocent passage can be performed within this zone without the express authorization of the concerned State. Again, attributing responsibility to the passive state on whose territory the interception is being carried out and not the actively intercepting State is justified by the numerous options at the disposition of the passive State that could have denied authorisation for such an interception and still carry the responsibility for interception itself, or proactively intercept the vessel further out the sea.[365]

The above situation seems crystal clear until Article 18 UNCLOS and number 97 of the ExCom's Conclusion are read in relation to the issue of authorisation. This Article states that; 'when vessels respond to persons in distress at sea, they are not engaged in interception'. Since such a scenario qualifies as a rescue mission and not an interception, the proposed ExCom rule cannot be applied. The

363 Andrew Brouwer & Judith Kumin, 'Interception and Asylum: When Migration Control and Human Rights Collide' (2003) 21(4) *Refuge* 6, analysing interception measures and effects.

364 Article 2(1) UNCLOS.

365 Article 2 (10 (3) UNCLOS.

situation is even cloudier given the uncertainty on whether the intervening State will request authorisation to disembark the rescued persons or whether it would treat them as intercepted persons. Recent observation shows that the line of action will depend on the interests and stakes of the concerned parties. This scenario further highlights the failure to address rescue disembarkation duties especially in relation to State military rescue. As a result, the protection duties and responsibilities of military maritime rescue deserve more academic, practical and diplomatic attention.

5.4.3 Interception in the Contiguous Zone

Nowadays, this contiguous zone permits States to exercise the control necessary to prevent or punish the infringement of their immigration laws and regulations despite the lack of clarity on the extent to which such control encompass interception is staggering.[366] But even if States are to conduct interception within this zone, there must be an identification of the State within whose sovereign territory or territorial waters the interception takes place, or cannot take place because the contiguous zone is not an area of complete State sovereignty. This limit of sovereignty in this zone has transformed it into a safe haven for numerous illegal activities thus justifying the increase in the number of interceptions and even more disturbing, interception is seemingly endorsed as legitimate in the Smuggling Protocol.[367] Unfortunately, the ExCom rule fails to address this as there is no application in the contiguous zone.

5.4.4 Interception in the High Seas

Similar to the contiguous zone, interceptions in the high seas are not addressed by the ExCom rules since the high seas do not fall within the State's sovereign territory. This situation literally saps the rules of their practical effectiveness and essence. As a matter of practicality, most States prefer to carry out interceptions in the high seas precisely to prevent vessels from entering their contiguous zone which is considered as the frontier of their territorial waters where greater protection duties are attached.[368]

In order to fully exploit this legal loophole, some States negotiate accords with neighbouring States to authorise them disembark foreign flagged vessels. The US Coast Guard even endorses high seas interceptions by observing that; 'interdicting migrants at sea means they can be quickly returned to their

366 Article 63 UNCLOS.

367 Article 8 (2) and (7) of the Smuggling Protocol.

368 Barbara Miltner, 'Irregular Migration – Refugee Protection Issues in Rescue and Interception' (2006) 30 Fordham Int'l. 125.

countries of origin without the costly processes required if they successfully enter the United States'.[369] This stance clearly does not favour the protection of the migrants at sea who stand the risk of being refouled to the danger they are coming from.

5.4.5 Land-Based Interceptions

The ardent desire to prevent migrants from reaching their targeted territories keeps extending its tentacles to unsuspected angles. It is no longer uncommon to find foreign immigration officers posted in airports to prevent onward travel by immigrants with false documents. This scenario technically implies that the intercepting State is acting from within the confines of the Venue State to block undocumented migrants from advancing towards their territory. Here, the ExCom rules heap the responsibility of protecting intercepted persons on the venue State and not the intercepting State acting on foreign land. The fact that land-based interceptions halt migrants within the territory of another State that is not the high seas entail that there is a high probability of refugees ending up trapped inside their country of origin. This poses a great problem especially where venue States constitute the State of origin rather than the State of transit.[370] Applying such a rule would render the State of origin responsible for the protection of persecuted persons trapped within its borders which is gravely incomprehensively.

5.4.6 A Way Forward-Supplementary Rules

From the above analysis, the ExCom rule appears to be undeniably efficient when the interception occurs within a State's territory since protection duties are simply assigned to the venue State; yet uncompromisingly inefficient in scenarios of interception that occur particularly in the high seas and the contiguous zone.

A plausible outlet to this inconvenience would be the drafting of supplemental rules to be applied *pari passu* the ExCom rules. A scholarly proposal in this line lays:

---

369 United States Coast Guard Office of Law Enforcement, Alien Migrant Interdiction: Overview (AMIO) <https://www.pacificarea.uscg.mil/Our-Organization/District-11/Response-Division/LE/Migrants1/(accessed/> accessed 30 June 2023.

370 By definition, a refugee must be outside of his/her country of origin in order to trigger protections under the Refugee Convention. However, while the inability to leave one's country does not violate Article 33 of the 1951 Refugee Convention, it is likely to constitute a violation of Article 12 ICCPR.

> For interceptions taking place beyond the sovereign territory or territorial waters of any State, including the contiguous zones and the high seas, the State exercising its jurisdiction over the interception has the primary responsibility for addressing any protection needs of intercepted persons.[371]

The above proposal should logically take charge of the legal silence observed by the ExCom rules on the responsibilities of States in the protection of migrants in zones beyond the sovereignty of the intercepting State. In summary, interceptions in zones with legal grey areas can be enshrined thus:

1. Responsibility for interceptions in a State's own contiguous zone goes to that State;
2. Responsibility for interception in a foreign contiguous zone with the permission of the passive State goes to the passive State because of the authorisation it granted;
3. Responsibility for interceptions on foreign jurisdiction without permission goes to the intercepting State;
4. The denial of authorisation and subsequent decision to intercept will attribute responsibility to the interceptor.

As concerns the high seas, the act of interception would trigger a corresponding duty to protect upon the intercepting State as the actor exercising its jurisdiction over the vessel. This may however lead to a decline in interceptions in the territorial seas as this is the sole maritime zone with explicit protection duties on the interceptor. This simply means that interception in the territorial sea is sanctioned by the imposition of protection duties that would not be possible if interception had been done in the high seas. This can be applied on both sea and land-based interceptions and may lead to an exponential rise in push-backs and high seas interceptions. Regardless of the maritime zone in which the interception occurs, the supplemental rule accurately attributes protection duties to the appropriate actors. This creates and equitable outcome for the stake-holders since the enjoyment of jurisdiction and power is married to the respect of duties which go a long way to protect the intercepted migrants.

One the major shortcomings of this rule is the inevitable possibility of encountering more than one State exercising jurisdiction over a particular zone like a situation where a flag State authorises a foreign flag State vessel to intercept. The outsourcing of interception to private entities by States is not an entirely absurd eventuality. Similar situations have already been witnessed

371 See note 40, page 49.

in the coast of Africa with the Somalian government contracting an American company to protect its coastlines from pirates.[372] There is equally the possibility of contracting foreign States to intercept in the high seas.[373] The above scenarios muddy the legal waters and render the legislation on interceptions even more onerous.

Despite the recent herculean efforts to strengthen refugee safeguards in rescue and interception, the results remain mediocre especially with the increasing percentage of migrant lives lost in the seas. The rescue context can however boast of a more efficient legal regime given the SOLAS and SAR amendments that further clarify aspects like disembarkation, rescue coordination and the delivery to a place of safety. Such legal certainty brightens a previously grey legal zone, thus restoring the viability and humanitarian practice that relies heavily on commercial vessels as its principal source of defence. The situation has remarkably improved despite the shortcomings of the legal arsenal.

The situation of interceptions demands even more attention despite the mammoth efforts by the ExCom Conclusion. Conceptual clarity remains a permanent dark cloud while the international protection duties need to be permanently attached to States in relation to their practices in the different maritime zones. The absence of distinct legal responsibilities of States in some maritime zones increases the number of interceptions in the high seas. Despite the proposal of supplemental rules, additional weaknesses remain like the absence of uniform procedural standards governing initial screenings for intercepted persons, and the deafening silence on the issue of extraterritorial detention, processing and protection arrangements. From practical and academic observation, the solutions to these bottlenecks impeding the effective protection of migrants at sea will require more intense scholarly, diplomatic and even military efforts to assist the UNHCR issue more comprehensive guidelines in the nearest future for the safety of human life.

372 BBC, 'US. Firm to Fight Somali Pirates' (25 November 2005) BBC News <http://news.bbc.co.uk/2/hi/africa/4471536.stm> accessed 30 June 2023.

373 When the private contractors failed to appear to protect the Somali coastline, the Somali government signed a contract with the U.S. Navy to provide assistance in protecting its territorial waters from pirates operating off its coasts, *see* BBC, 'U.S. to Help Tackle Somali Pirates' (17 April 2006) <http://news.bbc.co.uk/go/pr/fr/-/1/hi/world/africa/4915726.stm> accessed 30 June 2023. Although such an agreement demonstrates an exercise of Somali jurisdiction to allow the U.S. Navy to operate within its own territorial waters, such a scenario raises broader questions about the possibility of a state delegating its own high seas interception duties to another State, which raises novel jurisdictional issues.

Part 6: Application of Non-refoulement in Asylum Seeking

The ever-soaring volume of present-day migrants arriving by sea is a brutal reminder of the 'boat people' orchestrated by the Indochinese crisis in the seventies.[374] This reminder is even more petrifying due to the higher death-rates recorded as a result of the sorry sailing conditions while even more pathetic because of the relative weaknesses of international law and the consequent behaviour of concerned States. The consensual reaction of the international community to assisting the boat people exposed the weaknesses of international law in dealing with migrants at sea, notably asylum seekers.

Prominent among the litany of troubles experienced by asylum seekers are the decisions of States as to denying permission of entry into their territory mindful of the principle of non-refoulement. This issue arose mainly in relation to the treatment of those asylum seekers and refugees who possibly could be found among the migrants. The happy observation is the fact that the principle of non-refoulement applies to all migrants irrespective of their status or reasons for traveling by sea. The unfortunate truth is that not all migrants can be protected and treated in the same manner in the long run after the primary assistance and a place of safety has been provided especially with large scale arrivals. During the Indochinese crisis, the UNHCR Executive Committee affirmed that:

> It is therefore imperative to ensure that asylum seekers are fully protected in large-scale influx situations, to reaffirm the basic minimum standards for their treatment (...). In situation of large-scale influx, asylum seekers should be admitted to the State in which they first seek refuge and if that State is unable to admit them on a durable basis, it should always admit them at least on a temporary basis (...). In all cases the fundamental principle of non-refoulement including non-rejection at the frontier must be scrupulously observed.[375]

374 The Indochinese crisis specifically refers to the movement of refugees coming from the former French Indochina in consequence of armed conflict situations, as in Vietnam, and emergence of a dictatorial regime, as in Cambodia, *compare* A. Lakshamana Chetty, 'Resolution of the Problem of Boat People: The Case of A Global Initiative' (2001) 1 *ISIL Yearbook of International Humanitarian and Refugee Law* 144, 145.

375 Executive Committee, Conclusion No. 22 (XXXII) 1981; reaffirmed during the crisis in former Yugoslavia, in Executive Committee, Conclusion No. 74 (XLV) 1994.

It therefore becomes pivotal to determine the status of each and every migrant in order to gauge the ambits of assistance deserved. In this light, special attention should be given to the so-called non-entrée mechanisms implemented principally to prevent a refugee from having access to the procedures for determining his status.

Case law and practice testify that each arrival is different from the other. Therefore, there is a common aim underlying both the law of the sea and refugee law that can be combined in accounting for the security interests of the States as well as the protection of sea-borne asylum seekers.[376] Before examining the impact of interdiction programs on the protection of asylum seekers and refugees, it is crucial to re-establish the importance of non-refoulement in the protection of human rights regardless of status.

6.1 *The Importance of Non-refoulement in Protecting the Human Rights of Asylum Seekers*

Migration inevitably creates refugees and asylum seekers and they unavoidably suffer from human rights abuses. With the negligible focus on the push and pull factors causing migrations, the UDHR stipulates that '[e]veryone has the right to leave any country, including his own, and to return to his country'[377] and that '[e]veryone has the right to seek and enjoy in other countries asylum from persecution.'[378] Although the above provisions empower everybody to flee danger, they fail to oblige foreign countries to grant their territories as destinations for those fleeing. In the same light, the preamble of the 1951 Refugee Convention reiterates the contents of Article 14 UDHR, asserting that 'the individual does not possess a subjective right of asylum but he/she is merely entitled to request the status of a refugee and the required State has a discretionary power to accept or refuse the request'.[379]

This implies that asylum is an 'act of grace by States' and the refusals of States as to accepting an obligation to grant asylum is amply evidenced by the history of international conventions and other instruments.[380] Despite this discretion, preventing an individual from presenting the request can imply a

376 Seline Trevisanut, 'The Principle of Non-Refoulement at Sea and the Effectiveness of Asylum Protection' (2008)12 *Max Planck Y.B. U.N. L.* 205, 246.

377 Article 13(2) UDHR.

378 Article 14(1) UDHR.

379 Mark Pallis, 'Obligations of States towards Asylum Seeker at Sea: Interactions and Conflicts between Legal Regimes' (2002) 14 *International Journal of Refugee Law* 329, 341.

380 *Ibid.*, footnote 6.

breach of Article 14 UDHR in its meaning of a 'right to request' that is safeguarded by the principle of non-refoulement.

Given the ever-present threat of human rights violations faced by refugee and asylum seekers, the safeguards offered by the principle of non-refoulement have been enshrined in human rights law legislation like Article 3 of the Convention against Torture and other Cruel, Inhuman or Degrading Treatment or Punishment,[381] which prohibits the removal of individuals to States where they risk being subjected to torture or other inhuman or degrading treatment. According to the HRC a similar guarantee is offered by Article 7 ICCPR.[382] The non-refoulement principle is equally treasured in regional human rights documents like the ECHR in its Article 3, the American Convention on Human Rights of 1969 in its Article 22(8), and Article 5 of the 19981 African Charter on the Protection of Human and Peoples' Rights (Banjul Charter). Particularly worth citing is Article 45 of the 1949 Fourth Geneva Convention relative to the Protection of Civilian Persons in Time of War that states that 'in no circumstances shall a protected person be transferred to a country where he or she may have reason to fear persecution for his or political opinions or religious beliefs'.

Besides the above domains of international law that interact to provide a basis for a possible assertion of claims by asylum seekers, customary norms have developed to this effect such as that of 'temporary refuge' which prohibits forceful repatriation until violence ceases and the State can assure the security and protection of its nationals.[383] The notion of temporary refuge has gradually evolved into 'complementary protection' and can now be identified as 'temporary protection'. The evolution is consecrated in Europe by a Council Directive that provides:

> [T]hird-country nationals or stateless persons who have had to leave their country or region of origin, or have been evacuated in particular in response to an appeal by international organisations, and are unable to return in safe and durable conditions because of the situation prevailing in that country, who may fall within the scope of article 1 of the Geneva

381 A/RES/39/46 of 10 December 1984.

382 Human Rights Committee, General Comment No. 20 (1992), Doc. HRI/HEN/1/Rev.1 of 28 July 1994, para. 9.

383 Guy S. Goodwin-Gill and Jane McAdam, *The Refugee in International Law* (3rd ed. OUP 2007) 289.

Convention or other international or national instruments giving international protection, in particular:
i. persons who have fled areas of armed conflict or endemic violence;
ii. persons at serious risk of, or who have been victims of, systematic or generalized violations of their human rights.[384]

Despite the above legal and customary law arsenal in favour of refugees and asylum seekers, it should be noted that the connotation, perception and conception of temporary protection remains a vastly heterogeneous issue. Notable among these is the Australian approach that defines the granting of a 'temporal protection visa' permitting refugees who have entered unlawfully into the territory to stay, pending the determination of their status.

The pending conceptual precision of the concepts of non-refoulement and even temporal protection cannot be considered as impediments to the protection destined for asylum seekers, refugees and migrants by sea in general. On the contrary, the constant evolution of these concepts helps to broaden their scope and widen the ambits of protection available to this vulnerable group of migrants at sea unfairly unprotected for far too long now. It would however be naïve to abandon the evolution of these concepts to natural evolutions without constantly adapting and orientating the trends to blend with constantly changing state practices would hurt these rights. One of these practices is the interdiction program that is treated herein below.

6.2 *The Impact of Naval Interdiction Programs*

Despite the protection guarantees offered by the non-refoulement principle, contemporary State practices seem to undermine advancements. One of such practices is that of interceptions which as treated earlier above, comprises all measures applied by a State, outside its national territory, in order to prevent, interrupt or stop the movement of persons without the required documentation crossing international boarders by land, air or sea, and making their way to the country of prospective destination.[385] The most threatening of these practices is that of naval interdiction programs. The practice of naval

384 Council Directive 2001/55/EC of 20 July 2001 on Minimum Standards for Giving Temporary Protection in the Event of a Mass Influx of Displaced Persons and on Measures Promoting a Balance of Efforts between Member States in Receiving such Persons and Bearing the Consequences Thereof, OJEC No. L 212/12 of 7 August 2001.

385 UN High Commission for Refugees, Executive Committee, Interception of Asylum-seekers and refugees: The International Framework and Recommendation for a Comprehensive Approach, EC/50/CRP.17 of 9 June 2000, para. 10.

interdiction in the high seas consists of the action of one State or more, undertaken on the basis of an international agreement, aimed at exercising the right of visit in relation to criminal activities not listed in Article 110 UNCLOS,[386] performed by ships without nationality or by vessels sailing the flag of a State or a group of States. Most often, the interested flag State participates in the conclusion of the agreement. This is however not possible in the case of embargoes wherein; the interdiction program is aimed at sanctioning the flag State.[387]

The adoption of interdiction programs to prevent and obstruct irregular migrant flows, has become quite trendy in recent years. There exists a litany of interdiction programs,[388] but the most notorious worth examining is doubtlessly the United States' interdiction program with Haiti that was brought to the US Supreme court to determine its legality in relation to the right of asylum and the principle of non-refoulement. President Duvalier of Haiti concluded an agreement with the United States on the 23rd of September 1981 establishing 'a cooperative program of selective interdiction and return to Haiti of certain Haitian migrants and vessels involved in illegal transport of persons coming from Haiti'.[389]

Barely six days after the agreement, US President Reagan issued an executive order suspending the entry of irregular aliens coming from the high seas and ordered the coast guard to intercept vessels and to redirect them to their port of origin.[390] Aliens were screened on board the naval unit and those not eligible for refugee status were returned to Haiti. In just ten years, the US has

386 Article 110 UNCLOS provides the possibility for concluding such agreement: 'Except where acts of interference derive from powers conferred by treaty …', see also Angelos, M. Syrigos, 'Developments on the Interdiction of Vessels on the High Seas', in Anastasia Strati, Maria Gavouneli & Nikos Skourtos (eds.), *Unresolved Issues and New Challenges to the Law of the Sea* (Martinus Nijhoff 2006) 166 et seq.

387 Carl Q. Christol and Charles R. Davis, 'Maritime Quarantine: The naval interdiction of offensive weapons and associated material to Cuba' (1962) 4 *Journal of Inter-American Studies* 525.

388 The European 'pre-border operations' monitored by the European Agency for the Management of the Operative Cooperation at the External Boarders of the Member States of the European Union, FRONTEX Council Regulation (EC) 2007/2004 of 26 October 2004, OJEC No. L 349/1 of 25 November 2004; *see also* Seline Trevisanut, 'Europe and Irregular Migration by Sea: Frontex and International Law' (2008) *Diritto dell'Unione Europea* 367, 382.

389 Agreement to Stop Clandestine Migration of Residents of Haiti to the United States (1981) *International Legal Materials*.

390 Executive Order No. 12.324, *see* Marian Nash Leich, 'Contemporary Practice of the United States Relating to International Law' (1982) 76 *American Journal of International Law* 376 et seq.

exercised interdiction on over 25,000 Haitians. The US was however forced to suspend the interdiction programme in September 1991 after the fall of President Bertrand Aristide which saw a remarked increase in the number of arrivals from the Haitian island. The ever-increasing number of arrivals pushed the US government to restart the interdiction program the very next month with the US military base at Guantanamo used as a centre for the screening process. US President Bush then adopted in 1992 executive order 12.807, the 'Kennebunkport Order',[391] suspending the screening process and ordering the coast guards to redirect intercepted Haitians immediately. The famous Kennebunkport order constituted the claim against the US government tabled by two non-profit organisations before US jurisdictions.

Curiously, the Supreme Court judgement of 21 June 1993[392] did not find the actions of the coast guards illegal. This judgement confronted the principle of non-refoulement in several ways. But what is most import to note is the fact that the Court attempted to confer domestic legality on the practice of returning individuals to their country of origin, irrespective of their claim to have a well-founded fear of persecution. That decision did not and could not alter the State's international obligations.[393]

It should be noted that the US authorities violated the principle of non-refoulement by forcefully diverting intercepted vessels to their port of origin, thus preventing them from the possibility of seeking refuge in other countries of the region like Cuba, Jamaica or the Bahamas. It was on this basis that the bold-spirited Judge Blackburn founded his dissenting opinion by glaringly stating that;

> The refugees attempting to escape from Haiti do not claim a right of admission to this country [the United States]. They do not even argue that the Government has no right to intercept their boats. They demand only that the United States, land of refugees and guardian of freedom, cease forcibly driving them to detention, abuse, and death.[394]

391 The Kennebunkport Order was not modified by the successive US administration and thus it is still in force.

392 Supreme Court of United States, Sale v. Haitian Centres Council, Inc., 21 June 1993 (1993) 32 International Legal Materials 1039.

393 UNHCR, 'The Haitian Interdiction Case 1993 Brief amicus curiae' (1994) 6 *International Journal of Refugee Law* 85.

394 'Dissenting Opinion of Judge Blackmun' (1993) 32 *International Legal Materials* 1058 et seq.

The Supreme Court on the other hand discarded the application of Article 33 of the 1951 Refugee Convention beyond the territory of the State defending this approach, stating;

> If the first paragraph [of Article 33][395] did apply on the high seas, no nation could invoke the second paragraph's exception[396] with respect to an alien there: an alien intercepted on the high seas is in no country at all. If Article 33.1 applied extraterritorially, therefore, Article 33.2 would create an absurd anomaly: dangerous aliens on the high seas would be entitled to the benefits of 33.1while those residing in the country that sought to expel them would not.[397]

The basis of this conclusion was even pricklier given the narrow interpretation of the term 'return' in Article 33(1) invoking that;

> The French word 'refouler' encompasses terms as 'repulse', 'repel', 'drive back' and 'expel'. Thus 'return' means 'a defensive act of resistance or exclusion at a border rather than an act of transporting someone to a particular destination' and, in the context of article 33(1), it 'means to repulse rather than to 'reinstate' 1 5. But the term 'repulse' itself encompasses the term 'reject' and 'repel', actions not needing necessarily the prior entry into the territory. Consequently, to refuse to apply the principle of non-refoulement on the high seas seems to be unjustified'.[398]

Unsurprisingly, the UNHCR reacted to this decision in relation to the geographical scope of the principle of non-refoulement stating that:

395 Article 33(1) of the 1951 Refugee Convention 'No Contracting State shall expel or return ('refouler') a refugee in any manner whatsoever to the frontiers of territories where his life or freedom would be threatened on account of his race, religion, nationality, membership of a particular social group or political opinion'.

396 Article 33(2) of the 1951 Refugee Convention 'The benefit of the present provision may not, however, be claimed by a refugee whom there are reasonable grounds for regarding as a danger to the security of the country in which he is, or who, having been convicted by a final judgment of a particularly serious crime, constitutes a danger to the community of that country'.

397 United States: Supreme Court Opinion in Sale V. Haitian Centers Council (Right to Intercept and Interdict Haitian Refugees; UN Protocol Relating to Status of Refugees; U.S. Refugee Act of 1980) (1993) 32(4) *International Legal Materials* 1053.

398 Concetta Castrogiovanni, 'Sul refoulement di profughi haitiani intercettati in acque internazionali' (1994) *Riv. Dir.Int.* 474–478.

> The obligation not to return refugees to persecution arises irrespective of whether governments are acting within or outside their borders. UNHCR bases its position on the language and structure of the treaties' overriding humanitarian purpose, which is to protect especially vulnerable individuals from persecution. UNHCR's position is also based on the broader human right of refugees to seek asylum from persecution as set out in the Universal Declaration of Human Rights.[399]

In the same vein, it must be reiterated that the application of the principle of non-refoulement does not impute any hosting duties on the intercepting State or the State applying the interdiction program. Their principle obligation is not to preclude asylum seekers from seeking asylum elsewhere by forcing them back to their country of origin. Returning intercepted vessels back into the high seas may not necessarily imply a violation of the principle of non-refoulement, but forcing them back to their country of origin would undeniably constitute a violation of the principle of non-refoulement.

The brutal clarity of the American stance can be sharply contrasted with the European position despite the similarities portrayed by both in terms of policy objectives. In fact, joint patrols carried out the Mediterranean Sea within the framework of the EU agency Frontex[400] are exactly the same as interdiction programs except for their nomenclature, 'pre-border operations'. Frontex reports mention joint operations like HERA II and III,[401] charged with the interdiction of irregular migrant ships coming from Mauritania and Senegal, diverting them to their port of origin or to the Canary Islands when necessary. In fact, European units were even empowered to pursue their mission into foreign territorial waters, thus hindering migrant vessels from leaving Senegal and Mauritania. The HERA program saw the interception of close to 3887 illegal migrants as stated in the Frontex annual reports, but fails to state whether the intercepted migrants were submitted to a screening process by the patrols or in the countries they were redirected to.[402]

---

399 Notice of Other Recent Documents (Not Reproduced in International Legal Materials) (1993) 32(4) International Legal Materials 1215.

400 Joint patrols are organized pursuant to Article 3 of EC Regulation 2007/2004. FRONTEX Annual Report 2006, Coordination of Intelligence Driven Operational Cooperation at EU Level to Strengthen Security at External Borders 12.

401 Operation HERA started in July 2006 at the request of Spain because of the increasing number of arrivals of migrants by sea to the Canary Islands. Finland, Italy and Portugal participated at this operation with some naval units and aircrafts. Information concerning HERA and the other joint patrol programs carried on since 2006 under the supervision of the Frontex are available on the Agency website, frontex.europa.eu.

402 See note 27.

Despite the verbal shock expressed by the international community in relation to naval interdiction programs be they taken by the United States, Australia or the European Frontex programs, very little action has been taken to redress the situation. As a result, the final consequences for the asylum seekers remain precarious. Attention by the media and some interested governments has been morbidly focused on the prevention of arrivals and even grave, the sad lack of information and transparency regarding these operations. At least, it can be comfortably stated that migrants who are screened-in on the EU territory enjoy full procedural rights guaranteed by European law, while the unfortunate migrants intercepted or interdicted in the territorial waters of a third State during an interdiction program in the high seas, are subjected to the domestic laws of that State, considered safe by the European institutions.

The practice of forced redirection of asylum seekers in conclusion violates the right to seek asylum guaranteed by Article 14 UDHR and protected by the temporary refuge regime and the principle of non-refoulement, whose application in the different maritime zones, even in the high seas, cannot be challenged once States decide to exercise their sovereign powers.[403]

Part 7: Refugees at Sea – What Rights and Where?

The international and regional legal texts described above show that migrants at sea are treated differently from migrants arriving by land or air, and differently depending upon the nation in question. The above legal developments also demonstrate that migrants in distress at sea can benefit from a plethora of legal texts and doctrine that constitute a formidable arsenal. This well-articulated arsenal can be deployed to the advantage of refugees or migrants in need of protection, assistance or simply when applying a humanitarian approach to dealing with their situation. The legal arsenal however presents some fundamental weaknesses that substantially weaken compliance and the enforcement of these legal rules. These limitations include the absence of enforcement measures of legal obligations, uncertainty (ambiguity in interpretation of texts) in the duties of stakeholders after a rescue operation and the vagueness of facing criminal charges in the event of violating the treaty obligations. These shortcomings are examined individually below.

The lack of enforcement can be imputed first and foremost on the weak enforcement of international standards when dealing with vessels flying

403 Seline Trevisanut, 'Principle of Non-Refoulement at Sea and the Effectiveness of Asylum Protection' (2008) 12 *Max Planck Y.B. U.N. L.* 205, 246.

flags of convenience. Although the expression 'Flags of Convenience' is not mentioned in the UNCLOS or other maritime treaties, it is very common in practice and refers to cases in which ships are registered in, and fly the flag of States with which they do not have any relationship of ownership or other link. Consequently, such vessels are considered to be exclusively under the jurisdiction of the flag State.[404] In situations where the flag State is unwilling or unable to enforce existing standards, there is a likelihood that violations would certainly go unpunished and to the detriment of migrants at sea.

Another element that encourages non-compliance is the fact that the duties of a State in international law are not always translated into domestic law duties. In the case of the law of the sea, it can be noted that while some States have incorporated the duties mandated by UNCLOS, SOLAS and other treaties into their national laws,[405] some have vehemently held their grounds against any such incorporation.[406] The absence of incorporation has been quite detrimental because the accompanying sanctions for non-compliance with a duty remain unknown and unexploited unlike in cases where the incorporation is effectively done.[407] The absence of incorporation therefore relieves the masters of vessels and other stakeholders of their duties to provide assistance especially under domestic law. As a result, lack of incorporation into the domestic system eventually leads to lack of competence by domestic courts and logically the inadmissibility of claims related to the violation of the duty to rescue and even non-refoulement before these courts.

Lastly, the third hindrance to enforcement is related to the lack of jurisdiction of domestic judges. The protection of migrants can be severely obstructed by the lack of competence of national judges to hear cases on breach of duty to

---

404 Article 92 UNCLOS. The limited exceptions to the exclusivity of the jurisdiction of the flag State provided in UNCLOS and other treaties do not seem applicable in the case of non-compliance with the duty to rescue people in distress.

405 Italy has introduced rules on the duty to rescue in its Code of Navigation. According to Article 489 of the Code, it is compulsory to provide assistance to vessels in distress at sea, provided that assistance is possible without seriously endangering the rescuing vessel, its crew or its passengers. Masters are required to render assistance in all cases in which it may be reasonably expected that the operation will succeed and unless they have knowledge that assistance is being rendered by others, in conditions more appropriate or similar to those in which they would normally operate.

406 It should be mentioned here that this may be a duty under international instruments, such as Article 10(2) of the International Convention on Salvage, which requests States to 'adopt the measures necessary to enforce' the duty to render assistance.

407 In the case of Italy. Article 1185 of the Code of Navigation provides that the masters of national or foreign vessels, floating devices or aeroplanes who fail to render assistance are to be punished with exclusion for up to two years, which may rise to six years in the case of injury to persons and up to eight years in the case of death.

assist or on non-refoulement. This situation is aggravated by the quasi-absence of any international judge to hear such cases.[408] Despite the complex system of compulsory dispute settlement provided by the UNCLOS, it sadly envisages solely inter-State disputes.[409] This system entertains possible complaints for lack of assistance, probably by the State of nationality of those in need of assistance, most likely against the flag State or the coastal State.

Given the clearly identified duties of States and masters of vessels, it is very possible to envisage action on two separate grounds. This hypothesis is succinctly laid down by doctrine. The first action would be the violation of flag State's duty to oblige the master to save life. This can be qualified as lack of enforcement against masters who have breached this duty. The second would concern the duty of the coastal State to establish search and rescue facilities. In practice however, international relations between States would prevent them from antagonizing their relationship by indicting and prosecuting a ship captain in breach of his duty to save life at sea. Migrants in distress in the sea may sadly not possess very dissuasive tools to oblige ship masters to comply with their duties.[410]

Another lethal loophole with the legal regime on the protection of migrants at sea is the legal uncertainty surrounding the duties of State and vessel masters ensuing a rescue operation and evidently linked to disembarkation. In fact, the principal fear of the States and masters concerns the moment following a search and rescue operation that is directly linked to the fate of the persons recently rescued by the vessel. In line with SARS, these people should be delivered to a place of safety. Such delivery implies disembarkation which most often a matter of urgency given the likelihood of overcrowding in the vessel, absence or shortage of necessities and even commercial time-constraints. The persisting uncertainty on which State ought to accept disembarkation remains a thorn in the smooth and effective application of the duty to rescue.

Lastly, another negative factor on rescue operations that discourages even potential rescuers from proceeding to rescue migrants and asylum seekers at sea is the possibility of facing criminal charges. On several counts, the actors of a successful rescue operation who successively disembark their rescues in the port of a State besides that of the nationality of the saved persons, have been charged with the violation of domestic rules prohibiting illegal migration.[411]

408 With the possible exception of human rights courts.

409 Part XV UNCLOS.

410 Irina Papanicolopulu, 'The duty to rescue at sea, in peacetime and in war: A general overview' (2016) 98(2) *International Review of the Red Cross* 491–514, 503.

411 The German vessel Cap Anamur, after having saved thirty-seven people in the Mediterranean, had to moor for twenty-one days on the high seas close to the outer limit of

The simple act of bringing charges against such rescue masters seriously dents the good will of others with similar intentions given the time and pecuniary losses alongside a possible wages and even job loss they would incur during their detention pending trial. It would therefore be most welcome for States to amend their criminal legislation to exclude the levying of criminal charges on States and ship masters who were simply complying with their fundamental duties under the law of the sea.

Conclusion

The sea is a hostile environment and should not be challenged without adequate resources and preparation. Compelled by push and pull factors, thousands of migrants have braved the seas unprepared with sad results. In the last few decades, migrants in distress have literally transformed the sea into a cemetery with thousands of deaths notably in the Mediterranean. It is even more agonising to observe that fellow humans contribute extensively to this high death toll through discriminatory practices and policies which treat some migrants with lesser respect thus exposing them to greater danger and certain death.

This shocking fact has pushed the international community of States to fight the problems and challenges faced by migrants at sea. Basic human rights to life, movement and health of migrants at sea are regularly violated leading to massive death in the seas. In response, international instruments have been put in place to protect migrants at sea including: the United Nations Convention on the Laws of the Sea (UNCLOS), Safety of Life at Sea (SOLAS), International Convention on Maritime Search and Rescue at Sea (SAR), Security Council Resolution 2312 of 2016, Protocol Against the Smuggling of Migrants by Land, Sea and Air, the Prohibition and Prevention of Torture, Cruel and Inhuman Treatment or Punishment at Sea by the United Nations Convention Against Torture (UNCAT), the 1948 Universal Declaration of Human Rights (UDHR) and many others. This legal arsenal gives States, organizations, ship masters and even individuals the responsibility and duty to protect migrants at sea.

Italian territorial waters, before being allowed to call at an Italian port. The crew of the Cap Anamur, after being arrested for facilitating the illegal entry of migrants into Italian territory, were eventually released; *see* Tribunale di Agrigento, Judgment of 7 October 2009. On the case and the decisions by Italian judges, see Marco Cottone, 'Alcune notazioni in materia di reaticonnessiall'immigrazione clandestina via mare', in Amedeo Antonucci, Irini Papanicolopulu and Tullio Scovazzi (eds), *L'immigrazione irregolare via mare nella giurisprudenza italiana e nell'esperienza europea* (Giappichelli Editore Torino 2016) 85.

Worthy to note that the presence of these legal instruments does not guarantee the safety and protection of migrants at sea. Related concepts like refoulement and interception are interpreted with bias to implement discriminatory practices against certain migrants notably illegal migrants. The plight and fate of these sea migrants has become arguable one of the major humanitarian challenges of our time. It will be ethically shocking to validate institutional caprices to the detriment of fellow humans despite the material and human cost of saving migrants in danger of getting lost at sea.

It is therefore imperative for the international community to clarify the often complex and overlapping international obligations, thus improving the scale and scope of the instruments needed to ensure the effective protection of migrants at sea alongside effective cooperation.

Bibliography

Books

Barnes (Richard), 'The International Law of the Sea and Migration Control', *in*: Ryan (Bernard) and Mitsilegas (Valsamis) (eds.), *Extraterritorial Immigration Control: Legal Challenges*, Leiden, Nijhoff, 2010, pp. 103–149.

Basilien-Gainche (Marie-Laure), 'Leave and Let Die: The EU Banopticon Approach to Migrants at Sea', *in*: Moreno-Lax (Violeta) and Papastavridis (Efthymios) (ed.), *'Boat Refugees' and Migrants at Sea: A Comprehensive approach: Integrating Maritime Security With Human Rights*, Leiden, Brill Nijhoff, 2017, pp. 303–326.

Bastide-Burdeau (Geneviève), « Migrations clandestines et droit de la mer », *in*: La mer et son droit – Mélanges offerts à Laurent Luccini et Jean-Pierre Queneudec, Paris, Pedone, 2003, pp. 57–66.

Brouwer (Evelien), 'Extraterritorial Migration Control and Human Rights: Preserving the Responsibility of the EU and its Member States', *in*: Ryan (Bernard) and Mitsilegas (Valsamis) (eds.), *Extraterritorial Immigration Control: Legal Challenges*, Leiden, Nijhoff, 2010, pp. 199–228.

Caracciolo (Ida), 'Migration and the Law of the Sea: Solutions and Limitations of a Fragmentary Regime', *in*: Crawford (James), Koroma (Abdul G.), Mahmoudi (Said), and Pellet (Alain) (eds.), The International Legal Order: Current Needs and Possible Responses: Essays in honour of Djamchid Montaz, Leiden, Boston, Brill Nijhoff, 2017, pp. 274–287.

Chetail (Vincent), 'Sources of International Migration Law', *in*: Opeskin (Brian), Perruchoud (Richard) and Redpath-Cross (Jillyanne) (ed.), *Foundations of International Migration Law*, Cambridge, Cambridge University Press, 2012, pp. 56–92.

Chiara Locchi (Maria), 'The Mediterranean Sea as a European Border: Trans-Mediterranean Migration, Forced Return and Violation of Fundamental Rights', *in*: Vallet (Elisabeth) (ed.), *Borders, Fences and Walls*, Farnham, Ashgate, 2014, pp. 11–25.

Coppens (Jasmine), 'Interception of Migrant Boats at Sea', *in*: Moreno-Lax (Violeta) and Papastavridis (Efthymios) (ed.), *'Boat Refugees' and Migrants at Sea: A Comprehensive approach: Integrating Maritime Security With Human Rights*, Leiden, Brill Nijhoff, 2017, pp. 199–221.

Daillier (Patrick), 'Migrations et droit de la mer – Menace(s) en Méditerranée', *in*: Doumbé-Billé (Stéphane) et Thouvenin (Jean-Marc) (coordonnées par), Ombres et lumières du droit international: Mélanges en l'honneur du Professeur Habid Slim, Paris, Pedone, 2016, pp. 321–327.

Goodwin-Gillin (Guy S.), 'Setting the Scene: Refugees, Asylum Seekers, and Migrants at Sea – the Need for a Long-term, Protection-Centred Vision', *in*: Moreno-Lax (Violeta) and Papastavridis (Efthymios) (ed.), 'Boat Refugees' *and Migrants at Sea: A Comprehensive approach: Integrating Maritime Security With Human Rights*, Leiden, Brill Nijhoff, 2017, pp. 17–31.

Guilfoyle (Douglas), 'Transnational Crime and the Rule of Law at Sea: Responses to Maritime Migration and Piracy Compared', *in*: Moreno-Lax (Violeta) and Papastavridis (Efthymios) (ed.), *'Boat Refugees' and Migrants at Sea: A Comprehensive approach: Integrating Maritime Security With Human Rights*, Leiden, Brill Nijhoff, 2017, pp. 169–196.

Gutierrez Castillo (Victor Luis), 'The Struggle against Irregular Migration by Sea at the Canary Islands', *in*: Del Vecchio (Angela) (ed.), *International Law of the Sea: Current Trends and Controversial Issues*, The Hague, Eleven International Publishing, 2014, pp. 59–76.

Haddad (Emma), 'EU Migration Policy: Evolving Ideas of Responsibility and Protection', *Global Responsibility to Protect*, Vol. 2, 2010, pp. 86–100.

Klein (Nathalie), 'International Migration by Sea and Air', *in*: Opeskin (Brian), Perruchoud (Richard) and Redpath-Cross (Jillyanne) (ed.), *Foundations of International Migration Law*, Cambridge, Cambridge University Press, 2012, pp. 260–282.

Klein (Nathalie), 'A Maritime Security Framework for the Legal Dimensions of Irregular Migration by Sea', *in*: Moreno-Lax (Violeta) and Papastavridis (Efthymios) (ed.), *'Boat Refugees' and Migrants at Sea: A Comprehensive approach: Integrating Maritime Security With Human Rights*, Leiden, Brill Nijhoff, 2017, pp. 35–59.

Klug (Anja) and Howe (Tim), 'The Concept of State Jurisdiction and the Applicability of the Non-refoulement Principle to Extraterritorial Interception Measures', *in*: Ryan (Bernard) and Mitsilegas (Valsamis) (eds.), *Extraterritorial Immigration Control: Legal Challenges*, Leiden, Nijhoff, 2010, pp. 69–101.

Klug (Anja), 'Conclusion: Closing Remarks: The Present and Future of 'Boat Refugees' and Migrants at Sea', *in*: Moreno-Lax (Violeta) and Papastavridis (Efthymios) (ed.), *'Boat Refugees' and Migrants at Sea: A Comprehensive approach: Integrating Maritime Security With Human Rights*, Leiden, Brill Nijhoff, 2017, pp. 438–447.

Kneebone (Susan), 'Controlling Migration by Sea: The Australian Case', *in*: Ryan (Bernard) and Mitsilegas (Valsamis) (eds.), *Extraterritorial Immigration Control: Legal Challenges*, Leiden, Nijhoff, 2010, pp. 347–374.

Komp (Lisa-Marie), 'The Duty to Assist Persons in Distress: An Alternative Source of Protection against the Return of Migrants and Asylum Seekers to the High Seas?', *in*: Moreno-Lax (Violeta) and Papastavridis (Efthymios) (ed.), *'Boat Refugees' and Migrants at Sea: A Comprehensive approach: Integrating Maritime Security With Human Rights*, Leiden, Brill Nijhoff, 2017, pp. 222–247.

Moreno-Lax (Violeta) and Papastavridis (Efthymios), 'Introduction: Tracing the Bases of an Integrated Paradigm for Maritime Security and Human Rights at Sea', *in*: Moreno-Lax (Violeta) and Papastavridis (Efthymios) (ed.), *'Boat Refugees' and Migrants at Sea: A Comprehensive approach: Integrating Maritime Security With Human Rights*, Leiden, Brill Nijhoff, 2017, pp. 1–16.

Last (Tamara), 'Who is the 'Boat Migrant'? Challenging the Anonymity of Death by Border-Sea', *in*: Moreno-Lax (Violeta) and Papastavridis (Efthymios) (ed.), *'Boat Refugees' and Migrants at Sea: A Comprehensive approach: Integrating Maritime Security With Human Rights*, Leiden, Brill Nijhoff, 2017, pp. 79–116.

Lutterbeck (Derek), 'Irregular Migration and Immigration Control in the Mediterranean', *in*: Ureta (Ivan) and Lutterbeck (Derek) (ed.), *Migration, Development and Diplomacy – Perspectives from the Southern Mediterranean*, The Red Sea Press, Inc., Malta, 2008, pp. 127–145.

Obokata (Tom), 'The Legal Framework Concerning the Smuggling of Migrants at Sea under the UN Protocol on the Smuggling of Migrants by Land, Sea and Air', *in*: Ryan (Bernard) and Mitsilegas (Valsamis) (eds.), *Extraterritorial Immigration Control: Legal Challenges*, Leiden, Nijhoff, 2010, pp. 151–166.

Obokata (Tom), 'Boat Migrants as the Victims of Human Trafficking: Exploring Key Obligations through a Human Rights Based Approach', *in*: Moreno-Lax (Violeta) and Papastavridis (Efthymios) (ed.), *'Boat Refugees' and Migrants at Sea: A Comprehensive approach: Integrating Maritime Security With Human Rights*, Leiden, Brill Nijhoff, 2017, pp. 145–168.

Ryan (Bernard), 'Extraterritorial Immigration Control: What Role for Legal Guarantees?' in: Ryan (Bernard) and Mitsilegas (Valsamis) (eds.), *Extraterritorial Immigration Control: Legal Challenges*, Leiden, Nijhoff, 2010, pp. 3–37.

Zekri (Abderrazak), 'Migration and Development: Socio Economic Impact of Immigration in Tunisia', *in*: Ureta (Ivan) and Lutterbeck (Derek) (ed.), *Migration,*

Development and Diplomacy – Perspectives from the Southern Mediterranean, The Red Sea Press, Inc., Malta, 2008, pp. 1–15.

Articles

Adepoju (Aderanti), 'Formulating Migration Policy at the Regional, Sub-Regional and National Levels in Africa', *African Yearbook of International Law*, Vol. 16, 2008, pp. 25–52.

Attard (Felicity), 'Is the Smuggling Protocol a Viable Solution to the Contemporary Problem of Human Smuggling on the High Seas?' *Journal of Maritime Law and Commerce*, Vol. 47, 2016, pp. 1–20.

Awad (Ibrahim), 'Introduction: Concepts, Practice and Policies of International Migration in Africa', *African Yearbook of International Law*, Vol. 16, 2008, pp. 3–24.

Baldaccini (Anneliese), 'Extraterritorial Border Controls in the EU: The Role of Frontex in Operations at Sea', *in*: Ryan (Bernard) and Mitsilegas (Valsamis) (eds.), *Extraterritorial Immigration Control: Legal Challenges*, Leiden, Nijhoff, 2010, pp. 229–255.

Barnes (Richard), 'Refugee Law at Sea', *International and Comparative Law Quarterly*, Vol. 53, 2004, pp. 47–78.

Blake (Valarie), 'Mass African Migration into Europe: Human Rights and State Obligations', *Journal of Public Law and Policy*, Vol. 32, 2010, pp. 135–178.

Borelli (Silvia) and Stanford (Ben), 'Troubled Waters in the Mare Nostrum: Interception and Push-backs of Migrants in the Mediterranean and the European Convention on Human Rights', *Review of International Law and Politics*, Vol. 10, 2014, pp. 29–70.

Ceriani Cernadas (Pablo), 'European Migration Control in the African Territory: The Omission of the Extraterritorial Character of Human Rights Obligations', *International Journal on Human Rights*, Vol. 10, 2009, pp. 179–204.

Coppens (Jasmine) and Somers (Eduard), 'Towards New Rules on Disembarkation of Persons Rescued at Sea', *The International Journal of Marine and Coastal Law*, Vol. 25, 2010, pp. 377–403.

Coppens (J.), 'The Lampedusa Disaster: How to Prevent Further Loss of Life at Sea?' *The International Journal on Marine Navigation and Safety of Sea Transportation*, Volume 7, Number 4, December 2013, pp. 589–59.

Coppens (Jasmine), 'The Essential Role of Malta in Drafting the New Regional Agreement on Migrants at Sea in the Mediterranean Basin', *Journal of Maritime Law and Commerce*, Vol. 44, 2013, pp. 89–114.

Coppens (Jasmine), 'Migrant Smuggling by Sea: Tackling Practical Problems by Applying a High-Level Inter-Agency Approach', *Ocean Yearbook*, Vol. 27, 2013, pp. 323–358.

Delaney (Richard) and Wiggin (Jack), 'How the Coastal Migration Began', *EPA Journal*, Vol. 15, 1989, pp. 48–49.

Den Heijer (Maarten), 'Europe beyond its Borders: Refugee and Human Rights Protection in Extraterritorial Immigration Control', *in*: Ryan (Bernard) and Mitsilegas (Valsamis) (eds.), *Extraterritorial Immigration Control: Legal Challenges*, Leiden, Nijhoff, 2010, pp. 169–198.

Di Pascale (Alessia), 'Migration Control at Sea: The Italian Case', *in*: Ryan (Bernard) and Mitsilegas (Valsamis) (eds.), *Extraterritorial Immigration Control: Legal Challenges*, Leiden, Nijhoff, 2010, pp. 281–309.

Dominguez-Mujica (Josefina), Diaz-Hemandez (Ramon) and Parreno-Castellano (Juan), 'The Canary Islands' 'Maritime Wall': Migration Pressure, Security Measures and Economic Crisis in the Mid-Atlantic', in: Vallet (Elisabeth) (ed.), *Borders, Fences and Walls*, Farnham, Ashgate, 2014, pp. 27–50.

Expert Meeting on Refugees and Asylum-Seekers in Distress at Sea – How Best to Respond?, Djibouti, 8–10 November 2011, *International Journal of Refugee Law*, Vol. 24, 2012, pp. 485–497.

El Kot (Bashir), 'Illegal Migration in Libya: Problems and Solutions', *in*: Ureta (Ivan) and Lutterbeck (Derek) (ed.), *Migration, Development and Diplomacy – Perspectives from the Southern Mediterranean*, The Red Sea Press, Inc., Malta, 2008, pp. 115–126.

Ennaji (Moha), 'Intentions of Migration Among the Moroccan Youth', *in*: Ureta (Ivan) and Lutterbeck (Derek) (ed.), *Migration, Development and Diplomacy – Perspectives from the Southern Mediterranean*, The Red Sea Press, Inc., Malta, 2008, pp. 63–71.

Fernandez (Maïté), 'The EU External Borders Policy and Frontex-Coordinated Operations at Sea: Who is in Charge? Reflections on Responsibility for Wrongful Acts', *in*: Moreno-Lax (Violeta) and Papastavridis (Efthymios) (ed.), *'Boat Refugees' and Migrants at Sea: A Comprehensive approach: Integrating Maritime Security With Human Rights*, Leiden, Brill Nijhoff, 2017, pp. 381–407.

Frontex: Human Rights Responsibilities, *International Journal of Refugee Law*, Vol. 25, 2013, pp. 407–434.

Gammeltoft-Hansen (Thomas), 'The Perfect Storm: Sovereignty Games and the Law and Politics of Boat Migration', *in*: Moreno-Lax (Violeta) and Papastavridis (Efthymios) (ed.), *'Boat Refugees' and Migrants at Sea: A Comprehensive approach: Integrating Maritime Security With Human Rights*, Leiden, Brill Nijhoff, 2017, pp. 60–78.

Gammeltoft-Hansen (Thomas) and Tan (Nikolas F.), 'The End of the Deterrence Paradigm – Future Directions for Global Refugee Policy', *Journal on Migration and Human Security*, Vol. 5, 2017, pp. 28–56.

Gauci (Jean-Pierre) and Mallia (Patricia), 'The Migrant Smuggling Protocol and the Need for a Multi-faceted Approach: Inter-sectionality and Multi-actor Cooperation', *in*: Moreno-Lax (Violeta) and Papastavridis (Efthymios) (ed.), *'Boat Refugees' and*

Migrants at Sea: A Comprehensive approach: Integrating Maritime Security With Human Rights, Leiden, Brill Nijhoff, 2017, pp. 119–144.

Kilpatrick (Richard L. Jr.) and Smith (Adam), 'The International Legal Obligation to Rescue during Mass Migration at Sea: Navigating the Sovereign and Commercial Dimensions of a Mediterranean Crisis', *U.S.F. MARITIME LAW JOURNAL*, Vol. 28, 2015, pp. 141–194.

Kim (Seunghwan), 'International Law and Practice – Non-Refoulement and Extraterritorial Jurisdiction: State Sovereignty and Migration Controls at Sea in the European Context', *Leiden Journal of International Law*, Vol. 30, 2017, pp. 49–70.

Kirchner (Stefan), Geler-Noch (Katarzyna), and Frese (Vanessa), 'Coastal State Obligations in the Context of Refugees at Sea under the European Convention on Human Rights', *Ocean and Coastal Law Journal*, Vol. 20, 2015, pp. 57–82.

Kuruk (Paul), 'Asylum and the Non-Refoulement of Refugees: The Case of the Missing Shipload of Liberian Refugees', *Stanford Journal of International Law*, Vol. 35, 1999, pp. 313–350.

Markard (Nora), 'The Right to Leave by Sea: Legal Limits on EU Migration Control by Third Countries', *The European Journal of International Law*, Vol. 27, 2016, pp. 591–616.

Marrero Rocha (Inmaculada), 'The Implications of Spanish-Moroccan Governmental Relations for Moroccan Immigrants in Spain', *European Journal of Migration and Law*, Vol. 7, 2005, pp. 413–434.

Martin (David A.), 'Human Rights and Migration Management: Of Complexity, Balance, and Nuance', *American Society of International Law Proceedings*, Vol. 106, 2012, pp. 69–72.

McAdam (Jane) and Purcell (Kate), 'Refugee Protection in the Howard Years: Obstructing the Right to Seek Asylum', *Australian Year Book of International Law*, Vol. 27, 2008, pp. 87–114.

Miltner (Barbara), 'Irregular Maritime Migration: Refugee Protection Issues in Rescue and Interception', *Fordham International Law Journal*, Vol. 30, 2006, pp. 75–125.

Miltner (Barbara), 'The Mediterranean Migration Crisis: A Clash of the Titans' Obligations', *Brown Journal of World Affairs*, Vol. 22, 2015, pp. 213–238.

Mitsilegas (Valsamis), 'Extraterritorial Immigration Control in the 21st Century: The Individual and the State Transformed?', *in*: Ryan (Bernard) and Mitsilegas (Valsamis) (eds.), *Extraterritorial Immigration Control: Legal Challenges*, Leiden, Nijhoff, 2010, pp. 39–65.

Moreno-Lax (Violeta), 'Seeking Asylum in the Mediterranean: Against a Fragmentary Reading of EU Members States' Obligations Accruing at Sea', *International Journal of Refugee Law*, Vol. 23, 2011, pp. 174–220.

Moreno-Lax (Violeta), '*Hirsi Jamaa and Others v Italy* or the Strasbourg Court versus Extraterritorial Migration Control', *Human Rights Law Review*, Vol. 12, 2012, pp. 574–598.

Mutus Topraksevem (Ceren), 'Shared Responsibility in the Context of Extra territorialised/Privatised Migration Controls', *Queen Mary Law Journal*, Vol. 7, Special Conference Issue, Autumn 2016, pp. 123–124.

Neri (Kiara), 'Le droit International face aux nouveaux défis de l'immigration clandestine en mer', *Revue québécoise de droit international*, Vol. 26, 2014, pp. 123–154.

Noussia (Kyriaki), 'The Recue of Migrants and Refugees at Sea: Legal Rights and Obligations', *Ocean Yearbook*, Vol. 31, 2017, pp. 155–170.

O'Brien (S. Killian), 'Refugees on the High Seas: International Refugee Law Solutions to a Law of the Sea Problem', *Goettingen Journal of International Law*, Vol. 3, 2011, pp. 715–732.

Papassiopi-Passia (Zoe), Pasia (Eleni) and Varadinis (Dimitrios), 'Migration and Law: Greece', *Revue hellénique de droit international*, Vol. 67, 2014, pp. 1–68.

Papastavridis (Efthymios), 'Fortress Europe and FRONTEX: Within or without International Law', *Nordic Journal of International Law*, Vol. 79, 2010, pp. 75–111.

Powell (Eric), 'Taming the Beast: How the International Legal Regime Creates and Contains Flags of Convenience', *Annual Survey of International and Comparative Law*, Vol. 19, 2013, pp. 263–300.

Pugash (James Z.), 'The Dilemma of the Sea Refugee: Rescue without Refuge', *Harvard International Law Journal*, Vol. 18, 1977, pp. 577–604.

Pyeatt Menefee (Samuel), 'The Smuggling of Refugees by Sea: A Modern Day Maritime Slave Trade', *Regent Journal of International Law*, Vol. 2, 2003–2004, pp. 1–28.

Ratcovich (Martin), 'The Concept of Place of Safety: Yet Another Self-Contained Maritime Rule Or a Sustainable Solution to the Ever-Controversial Question of Where to Disembark Migrants Rescued at Sea', *Australian Yearbook of International Law*, Vol. 33, 2015, pp. 81–130.

Rios Rodriguez (Jacoba), 'Tension between Sovereignty and Human Rights in International Migration', *in*: UNIVERSITATEA TITU MAIORESCU, *Law between Modernization and Tradition. Implications for Legal, Political, Administrative and Public Order Organization*, Colloque de l'Université Titu Maiorescu de Bucarest, (21–23 avril 2015), Bucarest, Hamangiu, pp. 538–547.

Romashev (Y.S.) and Ostroukhov (N.V.), 'Migration by Sea: International Legal and Organizational Issues', *Journal of the Higher School of Economics*, Vol. 2016, 2016, pp. 149–165.

Schloenhardt (Andreas), 'Trafficking in Migrants in the Asia-Pacific: National, Regional and International Responses', *Singapore Journal of International and Comparative Law*, Vol. 5, 2001, pp. 696–747.

Spijkerboer (Thomas), 'Moving Migrants, States, and Rights: Human Rights and Border Deaths', *Law and Ethics of Human Rights*, Vol. 7, 2013, pp. 213–242.

Stephens (Dale), 'Comparative Approaches to Security and Maritime Border Control', *International Law Studies. US Naval War College*, Vol. 81, 2006, pp. 19–30.

Testa (David), 'Safeguarding Human Life and Ensuring Respect for Fundamental Human Rights: A Consequential Approach to the Disembarkation of Persons Rescued at Sea', *Ocean Yearbook*, Vol. 28, 2014, pp. 555–610.

Tical (George-Marius), 'Managing Migration as a Threat for European Union's Security', *European Journal of Public Order and National Security*, Vol. 2015, pp. 23–26.

Touba (Keltoum), « La traversée de la Méditerranée par les migrants: un radeau pour l'Eldorado … Une réflexion sur l'immigration méditerranéenne », *in*: Chiousse (Sylvie) et Labari (Brahim) (sous la direction de), *La Méditerranée à l'heure de la mondialisation*, Esprit Critique: Revue internationale de sociologie et de sciences sociales, Vol. 13, 2010, pp. 137–141.

Trevisanut (Seline), 'The Principle of Non-Refoulement at Sea and the Effectiveness of Asylum Protection', *The Max Planck Yearbook of United Nations Law*, Vol. 12, 2008, pp. 205–246.

Trevisanut (Seline), 'Recognizing the Right to be rescued at Sea', *Ocean Yearbook*, Vol. 31, 2017, pp. 139–154.

US Naval War College, 'Protection of Persons and Property at Sea and Maritime Law Enforcement', *International Law Studies Series*, Vol. 73, 1999, pp. 213–248.

Vacas Fernandez (Felix), 'The European Operations in the Mediterranean Sea to Deal with Migration as a Symptom: From the Italian Operation Mare Nostrum to Frontex Operations Triton and Poseidon, Eunavfor-Med and NATO's Assistance in the Aegean Sea', *Spanish Yearbook of International Law*, Vol. 20, 2016, pp. 93–118.

Wani (Ibrahim J.), 'International Migration and Human Rights', *African Yearbook of International Law*, Vol. 16, 2010, pp. 197–210.

Wilson (Brian), 'Human Rights and Maritime Law Enforcement', *Stanford Journal of International Law*, Vol. 52, 2016, pp. 243–320.

Conventions

Charter of Fundamental Rights of the European Union (2000/C 364/01).

Convention on the Rights of the Child, Adopted and opened for signature, ratification and accession by General Assembly Resolution 44/25 of 20 November 1989, entry into force 2 September 1990, in accordance with article 49.

European Convention on Human Rights, as amended by Protocols Numbers 11 and 14; Supplemented by Protocols Numbers 1,4,6,7,12,13,16. Entered into force on the 1st of June 2010.

International Convention on Civil and Political Rights, adopted on the 16th of December 1966.

International Covenant on Economic, Social and Cultural Rights, New York, 16 December 1966, entry into force, 3rd January 1976.

International Convention on Salvage, 1989 with Final Act London, 28 April 1989 (The Convention entered into force on 14 July 1996).

International Convention on Maritime Search and Rescue, Adopted in Hamburg, Germany on 27 April 1979.

International Convention for the Safety of Life at Sea, 1974.

Refugee Convention of 1951.

Universal Declaration of Human Rights.

United Nations Convention on the Rights of the Child.

United Nations Convention on the Law of the Sea.

United Nations Convention Against Transnational Organized Crime and the Protocols Thereto.

Protocol to Prevent, Suppress and Punish Trafficking in Persons, Especially Women and Children, supplementing the United Nations, Convention against Transnational Organized Crime; General Assembly resolution 55/25 of 15 November 2000.

Protocol against the Smuggling of Migrants by Land, Sea and Air, supplementing the United Nations Convention against Transnational Organized Crime, General Assembly resolution 55/25 of 15 November 2000.

www.ingramcontent.com/pod-product-compliance
Lightning Source LLC
Chambersburg PA
CBHW031327230926
51848CB00001B/123

* 9 7 8 9 0 0 4 6 8 5 0 9 3 *